NABEN RUTHNUM

CURRY

EATING, READING, AND RACE

COACH HOUSE BOOKS, TORONTO

first edition

 Canada Council **Conseil des Arts**
for the Arts **du Canada**

ONTARIO ARTS COUNCIL
CONSEIL DES ARTS DE L'ONTARIO
an Ontario government agency
un organisme du gouvernement de l'Ontario

Published with the generous assistance of the Canada Council for the Arts and the Ontario Arts Council. Coach House Books also gratefully acknowledges the support of the Government of Canada through the Canada Book Fund and the Government of Ontario through the Ontario Book Publishing Tax Credit.

LIBRARY AND ARCHIVES CANADA CATALOGUING IN PUBLICATION

Ruthnum, Naben, author
    Curry : eating, reading, and race / Naben Ruthnum.

(Exploded views)
Issued in print and electronic formats.
ISBN 978-1-55245-351-3 (softcover).

    1. East Indian diaspora. 2. East Indians--Ethnic identity. 3. East Indians--Race identity. 4. East Indians in literature. 5. East Indian diaspora in literature. 6. Ethnicity in literature. 7. Race in literature. 8. Curry powder. 9. Ethnicity. 10. Group identity. I. Title. II. Series: Exploded views

DS432.5.R88 2017   305.8914'11   C2017-904955-0

Curry is available as an ebook: ISBN 978 1 77056 523 4 (MOBI), ISBN 978 1 77056 524 1 (PDF).

for Kay Ruthnum

Introduction

I've only visited Mauritius, my particular old country, once. It was 1991, I was nine, and the visit turned into a funeral. Not my own — even though I did feel like I was dying while I sweated against the polyester chafe of the new Bart Simpson pyjamas my aunt had bought me during our London stopover.

My father, sister, and I had gone to Mauritius to visit my grandmother, discovering only when we arrived that she was terminally ill. Well, my dad and sister found this out, not me. I was too young to be involved. I was also relatively unconcerned; I didn't know her, having met her only once, as a toddler too young to form memories. The only recollection I have of being in my grandmother's presence took place shortly before her funeral, in her hospital room, where I pulled on the brim of my Bulls cap until my father took it off my head. We left a few minutes later.

I was shuttled off to my mother's relatives, and so missed the death that Dad didn't expect to deal with. Unequipped to face such seriousness, and isolated enough from this culture that I exhibited a juvenile version of cold, anthropological curiosity, I came back to a Hindu funeral: a pyre, torches. The only referent I had at that age was *Return of the Jedi*. A priest took a knife-swipe at a coconut balanced on my father's shoulder and missed. I laughed (a memory that still chills) and was shushed. Earlier, a tonsured chunk of hair had been taken out of my father's temple, exposing pale, veined skin. My unknown grandmother was wrapped in a sari, then wrapped in branches, then wrapped in flames. We left food offerings at the feet of temple gods, then, mysteriously, ate them after the funeral.

Before, or after, there was a curry. Vegetables, a thick sauce, rice that I couldn't get the knack of clumping and thrusting into the sauce with the bird-beak grip my uncles and cousins demoed for me. It had been forks and knives up until this day, as it would be afterwards. Tiny cuts I didn't know I had at the base of my cuticles tasted the curry as I did, the elements of sauce that bit my tongue taking purchase in the blood there, leaving a sting that lasted.

This is how books like these are supposed to start, isn't it? While it would be a little thin as a memoir, the material I have here would be excellent fodder for for a diasporic South Asian novel, one of many books in the genre about reconnecting to a homeland that makes sense of my alienated, Western childhood. But the brief account is incomplete, missing a key element: when I went back, I didn't have the revelatory homecoming or correction to a sense of loss that I've since read about in countless books – good ones, like Romesh Gunsekera's 1994 Man Booker finalist *Reef*, and stinkers like Kamala Nair's 2011 trope-ridden mini epic, *The Girl in the Garden*. There's no comfort or Truth to be found in my story of 'going home': only a series of incidents that revealed how isolated from the country of my family's origin, how Westernized, I was at the time and, in many ways, still am. The tactile details – the Bulls cap, the banana leaf, that curry meal that hurt my fingers and mouth – they're genuine, but on the page they become clichéd symbols in a story I've never wanted to write.

Curry isn't real. Its range of definitions, edible and otherwise, rob it of a stable existence. Curry is a leaf, a process, a certain kind of gravy with uncertain ingredients surrounding a starring meat or vegetable. It's an elevating crust baked around previously bland foodstuffs, but it's also an Indian fairy tale composed by cooks, Indians, émigrés, colonists, eaters, readers, and writers.

Fuck off, my ideal reader might be saying right now. *Of course it's real, it was on my plate and soaking into your naan last night.* And you'd be right, sort of. But even if the flavour is real, and delicious, it's also become a crucial element of how the story of South Asian cultural identity is told, in our mouths and on the page. It's a concept too large to be properly controlled by a recipe – the recommendations become descriptions of certain dishes, each push toward using hing or amchur an encouragement to use the same spice in a different dish, or to add so much turmeric that you permanently dye your roommate's white plastic cooking spoon.

Like wine, curry's mixture of definable qualities and conceptual breadth wields a metaphorical power. Paul Giamatti, playing a neurotic oenophile, has a small speech in Alexander Payne's 2004 film *Sideways* where he's talking about Pinot Noir but really talking about himself: 'It's thin-skinned, temperamental ... y'know, it's not a survivor, like Cabernet ... No, Pinot needs constant care and attention ... Only somebody who really takes the time to understand Pinot's potential can then coax it into its fullest expression.' I remember being irritated by this transparently symbolic dialogue in a movie I'd been enjoying, though in later viewings it seems to me that the script and Giamatti's character, Miles, know exactly who is being spoken about through the wine, that the personal symbolism of Pinot is a rooted part of Miles's personal myth, one he repeats to himself and to anyone who asks him and cares to listen.

Curry can, and often does, tell a similarly loaded story, but one that goes beyond emphasizing aspects of a single persona: it carries a weight of meaning across the immense and indefinable South Asian diasporic culture. The familiar flavour is an aromatic but invisible link between the writer and the reader, the cook and the eater. In the steadily building mass of South Asian diasporic writing and discussion of identity, curry is an abiding metaphor for connection, nostalgia, homecoming, and distance from family and country. This collection of dishes covers a lot of metaphorical ground. It relies on a non-specific blend, a combination that can be adjusted and spun multiple ways, and yet carries identifiable defining top and bottom notes of flavour. The exact ingredients often aren't clear to anyone but the cook, and sometimes not even to him or her – the Indian ammas of recipes and diasporic novels are notorious for their freehanded dashes and pinches of ingredients, and the first- or second-generation protagonists of these novels are consistently grasping for a sense of identity and place as they try to get the recipe right.

Eating, reading, and remembering are all activities that begin domestically, perhaps especially in diasporic households, where home life can be all of life for kids who don't insist on spending time outside or with friends in unregulated, non-learning-related activities. In the spirit of a book about curry and reading, I should be making a comparison between the bookshelves and the spice rack of a diasporic household, but there's a crucial difference. I got to choose what I read when I was a kid, but not what I ate. From the outset, I avoided books with Indian names on the cover, with tangles of red silk and those fonts that designers love sticking above a picture of a banyan tree and a scattering of cardamom seeds. I demanded a justification for why we – amend that *we* to my parents; I wasn't buying anything – bought so many of these books written by people from a country my parents hadn't even grown up in, or visited. They didn't bother offering an answer to my questions, which were, more truthfully, attacks. The back-cover copy on these volumes was, if not identical, repetitive. Well into my teens, I'd always opt for Roth over Rushdie, Nabokov over Narayan.

Stories about reading are necessarily stories about prejudice: forming reading habits means cultivating strict prejudices and then carefully discarding them. As the posters in the kids' section at the library inform us, reading can take you anywhere. But damned if you're not going to decide exactly where and when you want to go. Much of the research for this book derived from books that had arrived in my hands over the years and articles that had flitted into my feed: reading outside the classroom is about controlling the accidental arrival of information, turning a chaotic flow of words and stories into an organized system of taste through rejection.

My family had a strict rule against reading at the table, the given logic being that it forced blood to your brain that should properly be in the gut, aiding digestion. My parents both being medical professionals (an ophthalmologist and a psych nurse), I didn't challenge this logic.

We ate with the news on, and only rarely was the nightly meal not Mauritian food, which I'd describe to friends as Indian food as a shorthand to leave out the explanation of Mauritius being an island off the east coast of Africa, and later just describe, self-mockingly, as 'Curry, what else would we eat?' anticipating and cutting off jokes from the fairly unprogressive Western Canada youth of the 1990s. I loved the stuff, anyway. I accepted it and defended it as part of my cultural identity, an easily identifiable and likeable part of it, one in which I had built-in, extremely fake expertise. Any time a white friend reported his mom or dad making a curry with coconut milk or snap peas in it, I dismissed it as 'the white man's curry,' and was at least correct in that neither ingredient was common in the Mauritian curries that were made in my house.

Curry was a territory I defended, an absolute truth based on the way it was made in my family's kitchen, despite the delicious counterarguments we ate at restaurants in Vancouver (and eventually even in Kelowna, the expanding small city in British Columbia where I grew up). There was an acceptable authenticity in what we ate, one I felt ran counter to the books with various brown hands, red fabrics, clutched mangoes, and shielded faces that turned up on our shelves with such regularity that we may have been members of some Columbia House Diasporic Novel subscription package that none of us knew how to cancel. My family enjoyed the books, and continue to read some of them. In doing research for this volume, I had to expand beyond my usual method – picking up books that interest me and finding connected texts. I asked a close relative if she had any recommendations for – as I put it in the email – 'super-typical "I miss the homeland" novels you've read by South Asian authors in the past few years.' She replied, 'Oh God, I avoid these like the plague. My white friends seem to enjoy them.'

They do indeed – so do some of my white friends, and their parents. But so do some of my brown friends, and their parents. I've read quite a few of these books by now, both by accident and on determined purpose for this book, as I've tried to hew out exactly what I've had in mind when my teenaged self defined these novels that I avoided as 'currybooks': it's certainly not a description I'd apply to absolutely any book from the vast output of diasporic authors, or authors still based in India. Anita Desai's work, Salman Rushdie's, Hari Kunzru's, Michael Ondaatje's – it doesn't linger in the nostalgic, authenticity-seeking reconciliation-of-present-with-past family narratives that are endemic to what I call currybooks. They don't follow the genre rules, even if they nip in and borrow here and there. They exist as reflections of the author's consciousness and culture, with culture processed through that consciousness. For example, Rushdie's continual seeking of the truth outside of realism is exactly how he escapes tropes before they can solidify: his own recollection of India in *Midnight's Children* had to acknowledge the existence of an India-of-the-mind, constructed from recall. And Anita Desai's vision, in books such as *In Custody*, is as connected to the stylistic work of authors such as Henry James and Edith Wharton, with whom she presumably went through that whole anxiety-of-influence thing that writers do, as it is to the places where she grew up and the work of Indian authors such as R. K. Narayan.

Food and literature are the defining elements of the way I see myself in the Indian diaspora in the small world I've built around myself as a brown adult in the West: curry's the vehicle I use to look at how we eat, read, and think of ourselves as a miniature mass-culture within the greater West. Curry's just as fake and as real as a great novel, as a sense of identity.

Like the English language, curry is a colonial endpoint: everything ended up in it, and it remains infinitely changeable, even as its complex colonial roots became disguised as homeland authenticity. The tikka masala–inventing cooks at Indian restaurants in the 1970s gave Indian, Pakistani, and Bangladeshi immigrants a tasteable identity – a primarily British public encountered these people from the saucy, spicy dishes that would seem out of place in the homeland kitchens of these émigré chefs. What the Brits were really eating was the improvisations of various chefs. Tikka masala's (disputed) origin: a Pakistani restaurateur in Glasgow added some tomato sauce to the meal of a bus driver who was complaining that his food was dry. Without abandoning the spices on the rack and the colonially informed cuisine they grew up with, the immigrant cooks of Great Britain shaped a cuisine that is definitive of eating out, and carry-out, in the U.K.

Even the most commonly understood characteristic of curry came to be by way of the machinations of international trade and colonialism. Curry has many immutable qualities, but no definition of the dish can escape heat, or at the very least the potential for heat. This central characteristic is what prompts diners to say, 'It's not too hot, is it?' or 'Make it actually hot, not just medium, I can take it,' to bored waiters in Indian restaurants all over the world. Though it is a truly difficult fact for many Indians and children of Indian immigrants to acknowledge, chilies are not native to India at all – they were actually brought to the subcontinent from the Caribbean in the fifteenth century, by way of the trade-savvy, empire-hungry Portuguese.

It's slightly identity-shaking to me – and perhaps to any brown person who wasn't previously aware of the history – to find out that chilies were planted on our shores by some spice-route jagoff. Lizzie Collingham's superb 2005 book *Curry* (subtitled *A Biography* in the U.K. and *A Tale of Cooks and Conquerors* in North America) is committed to drawing out the historical truths that shaped the elusive identity of curry. Indian recipes, including ones in the vast curry family, have been adapted or altered to suit rulers, visitors, and colonial intruders for hundreds of years – with pulao rice arising from Persian pillau rice, and with creams and spices being increased or decreased in various dishes to suit the increasingly adventurous palates of British Raj occupiers. The Bangladeshi, Indian, and Pakistani immigrant cooks in 1970s England who added tinned tomatoes, ginger, garlic, and chili to tandoor-forged chicken to make tikka masala weren't undoing centuries of tradition: they were innovating and adapting a living cuisine that has sustained itself not by pandering to foreign cultures, but by absorbing them. The inauthenticity of curry is its greatest claim to its position as a reflection of global history and the present politics of hunger, eating, and identity.

As the resource-leeching rule of the British began to wane in India, a parallel distaste for food from India took place in the U.K. Curries, exotic to some Brits and a powerful reminder of youth and childhood to thousands of whites who'd grown up or spent their career years working for the Empire abroad, fell out of fashion for a while. Collingham points to a post-Victorian backlash against curry due to its supposed unsuitability to middle-class British stomachs and the powerful smells attendant on its preparation. But curry had threaded as deeply into England as the English language had reached into the colonies. The influx of Indian, Bangladeshi, and Pakistani immigrants of the mid-twentieth century made the ingrained British taste for a food that had been part of their own national history impossible to ignore, and curry made its comeback. 'By 1970 there were two thousand Indian restaurants in Britain,' Collingham writes. This number has since climbed to about 12,000, with estimated sales of £4.2 billion.

The food served in these establishments as late-twentieth-century U.K. Indian cuisine took shape often had little to do with what the cooks ate at home. For their children, this wasn't the case. In an interview Collingham quotes, landmark British restaurateur Haji Shirajul Islam discusses how he didn't eat the curries his restaurants prepared, but that his son's palate quickly took a British turn: 'When he goes to the restaurant he eats Madras – hot one … Me I always eat in the house. When I offer him food he eats it, but he says it's not tasty like restaurant food, because he's the other way round now.' As Lizzie Collingham concludes: 'For generations of British customers, and even second-generation Indians, the vindaloos and dhansaks, tarka dhals and Bombay potatoes, *are* Indian food.'

As a first-generation Mauritian-Canadian, eating salmon and chicken curry and smelling it as it cooked were the earliest markers of my difference growing up, though I had to go outside and make white friends to truly find that out. In Kelowna, where I spent my childhood and teen years, I was twice literally asked what colour my blood was in a friendly, genuinely curious tone. Even as a child, I noticed the noticing, the whipped-around heads at the melanin flood my family represented when we entered any public space in 1980s Kelowna. Food supplies were also a problem: key ingredients for curry and other Mauritian meals had to be picked up on weekend missions to Vancouver, the nearest city with a significant population of South Asian transplants. For a few years, garam masala was shipped directly to us from Mauritian family in packages that leaked a powerful odour no matter how well they'd been wrapped. Curry travels along with the diaspora, continuing the long trip of its evolving existence. The range of variations on curry dishes just across the subcontinent, leaving out islands like Mauritius and Guyana, or significant outposts of diasporic Indians such as South Africa, is staggering. I can still go to an Indian restaurant and taste something made with ingredients that are entirely Indian but quite foreign to me. I had chicken chettinad and tasted the cinnamony tree-lichen kalpasi just a few months ago. It makes perfect sense that I'm unfamiliar with many Indian dishes: I learned them all from restaurants and books over here. From an early age, my parents made me aware that there were minor and major differences between Mauritian and Indian food, even if they didn't provide a detailed explanation. Something to do with ginger and the Chinese population on the island, the story would start, before deviating into an anecdote about Chan, the man who ran the corner grocery on the street where my father grew up. Curry stories have a propensity for tipping into the nostalgic.

Curry is not a cliché. Well, maybe it is. The unifying notion of curry as an authentic, homeland-defining collection of dishes that form a cultural touchstone for diasporic brown folks is a cliché, in the same way food-based bonds between people from any culture who find themselves in a new land is a cliché. But curry can't be trapped. If you push through the cliché, you arrive at a surprising truth: the history of this ever-inauthentic mass of dishes is a close parallel to the formation of South Asian diasporic identity, which is as much of a blend of conflicting cultural messages forced into coherence as Indian cuisine itself.

Then again, the entire category of food writing comes with built-in nostalgia, a resurrection of remembered meals that, at its best, creates hunger to recreate that experience. When the topic, or the writer, is associated with a certain ethnic background, that act of nostalgia is positioned as a cultural act of looking-back. The *New Yorker*'s Adam Gopnik splits the food-literature genre into two categories:

There are two schools of good writing about food: the mock epic and the mystical microcosmic. The mock epic (A. J. Liebling, Calvin Trillin, the French writer Robert Courtine, and any good restaurant critic) is essentially comic and treats the small ambitions of the greedy eater as though they were big and noble, spoofing the idea of the heroic while raising the minor subject to at least temporary greatness. The mystical microcosmic, of which Elizabeth David and M. F. K. Fisher are the masters, is essentially poetic, and turns every remembered recipe into a meditation on hunger and the transience of its fulfillment.

Food writing is also memoir, at least outside the confines of the newspaper restaurant review. The alimental is elemental to a life story. M. F. K. Fisher's rapturous descriptions of meals in France are also the story of an adventurous American woman abroad, eating, writing, and living in quaint circumstances with a husband or between marriages. A great portion of Fisher's and Elizabeth David's writing deals with food and food experiences in France and continental Europe, an ongoing suggestion to readers that real food was something that existed elsewhere, not in the country of the writer's origin (America and England, respectively). Fisher's adventurous trip to isolated restaurants in Burgundy, where she's served pickled herring that is 'mild, pungent, meaty as fresh nuts,' and trout served *au bleu*, gutted and cooked half-alive in bouillon, 'agonizingly curled on a platter,' is as much about the hidden chef and the exuberant server, the sense of being alone and given a unique gift in a foreign land, as it is about the food, which Fisher actually describes in rather quick little clauses, compared to the considerable time given to describing the 'mad waitress,' 'fanatical about food like a medieval woman possessed by the devil,' and her own sensations of hunger, surfeit, determination, and even fear in the face of an epic meal. There are certainly exceptions to this questing-in-a-foreign-land in each writer's oeuvre, from Fisher's paean to Old Mary the cook's peach pie at the family's California ranch, to David's *English Bread and Yeast Cookery*. But Fisher's rapturous descriptions of French meals and life and David's landmark recipe books *Mediterranean Food* and *French Provincial Cooking* established their reputations and carried a clear message: the truest experiences of eating are out there, *là-bas*, and the amateur cook's hopeless task is to try to create the real thing at home.

In the case of Elizabeth David's early books and columns, the tasks assigned by the recipes were actually impossible fantasies – many of the ingredients her recipes required, like lemons and eggplant, were near-impossible to obtain in rationed Britain. This narrative of the real, right thing being elsewhere, particularly Continental Europe, has echoed through the biographies and restaurants of many American chefs, even in decades where French cuisine fell slightly out of fashion on the other side of the Atlantic. Both Anthony Bourdain in *Kitchen Confidential* and Bill Buford in his chronicle of life in Mario Batali's kitchen, *Heat*, describe chefs turning away from the complexities of French cuisine to the purity of Italian regional cuisine, made properly (which, to Batali, meant made by chefs who had trained in Italy with real Italian cooks with access to old-world knowledge). The supposed cleansing effect that this turn to the authenticity of another country may not have changed American haute cuisine forever, but it certainly impacted the 'story' of these particular chefs, bringing notoriety to their cuisine and personas.

When a food writer is a South Asian immigrant, or even a few generational steps from the plane or boat, another ripple enters. One of the conventions of diasporic food writing dictates that the writer's identity and self-discovery are implicitly linked to a tracing-back of culinary roots, a finding-out of who he or she really is in the rich smell of a Keralan masala finally nailed. That's the extra dimension to writing about curry and other ethnic foods: beyond meditating on hunger and fulfillment, writing about curry and India and the real food of one's ancestors becomes a meditation on personal and familial identity, and its relationship to the place where one grew up, or where one was wrested away from. The inability of the writer to reproduce his or her mother's aloo gobi often becomes, as if by default, a metaphor for the impossibility of full communication between generations – a metaphor so overwrought it's now as codified and recognizable as a Noh mask.

In 'The Long Way Home,' a 2004 essay for the *New Yorker*, Pulitzer Prize–winning Indian-American novelist Jhumpa Lahiri contributes to this form of writing that connects family, roots, secrets, and the lost unknowables of the past incarnated in particular delicious dishes. In Lahiri's case, her mother had learned to cook by witnessing and participating in her own mother's cooking in Calcutta, learning lessons that she carried to America by, for example, getting 'down on the floor to pound turmeric or chilies on a massive grinding stone.' Lahiri's mother here joins a line of mothers in this food-writing tradition. Like so many before her, she kindly evades sharing their recipes, never records or verbally details them: 'To this day, if friends ask how she made a particular dish, she cryptically replies, "It's nothing, really, you simply take all the ingredients and put them in the pot."' This reluctance to share methods is perhaps true of many mothers, and extremely common in these nostalgic essays and stories. My mother, thankfully, will give up any recipe, with detailed directions. Lahiri ends up learning her Indian-cooking techniques from a cookbook by Madhur Jaffrey, doyenne of subcontinental cookery books and TV since the early 1970s. In the end, her mother is quietly impressed, taking a photo of the spread that Lahiri and her sister make for their parents' thirtieth anniversary.

In 2016, Scaachi Koul contributed to the genre with an essay for BuzzFeed on learning how to cook the dishes of her childhood as an adult, 'There's No Recipe for Growing Up':

> My mom had watched my grandmother cook for years, knew her languages, knew how to pleat a sari or mutter a Kashmiri insult ('*Thrat*') or throw a wedding for her son, 25 years after she moved away. I don't have any of these secrets, because I was born in North America and raised around white people in a family that wanted to integrate. So it felt important to at least try to remember how my own mom did things.
>
> Late last week, I called my mom to get a refresher on a few of her recipes. I wanted to make rogan josh, aloo gobi (potatoes and cauliflower), chicken biryani (chicken and rice), and paneer with palak (spinach). But my mom, like so many Indian mothers I know, has always avoided giving me complete recipes.

Mothers are an important and authentic part of the curry genre, both cooked and written: not only a source of accessible, cross-cultural nostalgia, but a reminder that there are domestic, comforting aspects to exoticism. The parental link to the homeland, especially for writers with immigrant parents who themselves were born in the West, or who moved to the West at such a young age that their grasp on the old country remains light, questioned by brown people who dismiss their experiences or white people who say, 'But you seem so *white*,' can also have a sinister, minimizing aspect. If mothers are baggaged with the symbolic weight of a motherland and the author's distance from this place and identity, they sometimes aren't given much room of their own to be intact characters themselves. Mothers are permitted to be mysterious or generous in this system of symbolism, but in Lahiri's essay, her mother's pattern of selective withholding becomes her primary trait. And Lahiri, the writer, is burdened with mastering the domestic skill of cooking in order to achieve an understanding and connection with her mother. In Koul's piece, being able to cook her mother's food comes to stand in for her need for her mother's love and presence: Koul manages to pull off cooking a solid meal, catching the intangible scents of her mother's kitchen while she prepares it, but the meal 'wasn't as good because my food, as surprisingly palatable as it was, didn't include my mom hovering over me with a wooden spoon.' For these writers, their personal relationships with their mothers overwhelms the symbolic stand-in of mother for motherland, of food and the ability to prepare it properly as a marker of authenticity: but for many readers, this may not be the case – the mother on the page remains a symbolic stand-in for authenticity lost, despite the writer's labour to own the metaphor, to make it personal.

In part, these two pieces reflect ways I've found myself thinking about my race and family, and even writing about these matters … at least until I stop myself out of fear that I'm replicating an essay that already exists. That this treatment of a relationship between food, family bonds, and a fraying connection to the homeland appears frequently in essays and novels by diasporic South Asians doesn't invalidate it. An oft-repeated story isn't a false one: experiences and dishes like the ones described by Koul and Lahiri take place in the kitchens of brown undergraduates worldwide. The two essays above hit many of the same points about authenticity, love, and the unknowability of one's parents, but stylistically they are distinct to their authors, and there is no sense that the details are anything but true, lived experience. I mean, I've had a bunch of those experiences, too: a recipe is given over the phone, but a half pound of burnt onions and candied-walnuts-subbing-for-almond-slivers later, there's a stovetop of muck that has nothing to do with home, comfort, or good food. Just failure, distance, a sense that something essential has been lost. This is authentic, isn't it? It's also relatable, to readers from any number of immigrant backgrounds. So why shouldn't it be written about?

It should be, of course. Stories beget similar stories, and they don't become lies as a result. But endless encounters with one narrative – one that tells us that truth and colonialism are embedded in these family recipes and our failures to cook them – make me wonder why I keep reading this particular story over and over again, and why white and South Asian publics alike embrace it. South Asian food came to major prominence in the West with the explosion of Indian restaurants in the U.K., and the formative wave of South Asian diasporic writers followed soon afterward. When genres and forms have been around for long enough, there comes a point when they risk calcifying: becoming the same stories. This narrative thread, this way of thinking about curry, is one iteration of what Chimamanda Ngozi Adichie recently called 'the single story,' one overarching narrative that 'creates stereotypes, and the problem with stereotypes is not that they are untrue, but that they are incomplete. They make one story become the only story.'

Thinking about and writing about a food as culturally complex as curry as though it were a marker of an authentic past that is now lost, or a signifier of a broken bond between generations due to geographical dislocation, does a major disservice to how delicious curry is, and to how particular a South Asian diasporic experience can be.

Let me tell you about two personal curries of note. The logic of this genre dictates that if I describe a beloved dish, I'll be describing myself, achieving insight into family bonds, reaching back through a sense of the past into a concrete known this-much-is-true exchanged in knowing looks over bites of curry and rice. If it doesn't work out, you'll at least emerge with an excellent, usable recipe.

First, the chicken curry that I make a few times a month, from a now-freehanded recipe liberally adopted from Vikram

Vij's first cookbook, modified by my own tendency to favour coriander and turmeric. Vij built his small, fusion-friendly Indian restaurant in Vancouver into a national brand, eventually opening a wallet-friendly companion restaurant, a fleet of cookbooks and frozen meals, and standing in judgment on Canada's version of the entrepreneurial pitching show *Dragons' Den*. In the restaurant's first cookbook, written by Vij's ex-wife, collaborator, and business co-owner, Meeru Dhalwala, this recipe is set up with a brief tale of parents and the diaspora: 'This was the original chicken curry Vikram's mom used to make in his apartment when he first opened Vij's in 1994 and didn't have the appropriate licences to cook in the newly acquired cafe. This curry is based on a family recipe, except that she added sour cream to make it richer.'

I take some trendily twenty-first-century licence of my own by throwing in torn-up kale leaves as the curry approaches the end of its simmer: an effective way of vanishing greens under the vivid yellow creaminess of this sour cream–aided sauce, which acts as a subtle delivery model for the red powder hiding deep in the masala. The introduction of sour cream into a curry, by the way, wouldn't be entertained in the home I grew up in. Yogourt, sure, but not sour cream. I like it and think it works pretty well in this dish, though I often forget to stir a bit of masala into the sour-cream container to bring the temperature up before dumping the whole thing into the pot, which leads to a distastefully curdled appearance that guests are usually too kind to comment on.

This dish is mine now, based not just on the addition of kale but on one of the great strengths of curry: its flexibility, its demand that you freehand ingredients. The original recipe is precise, down to the ½ tsp ground black pepper. Mine has a handful of black pepper generous enough to blind a bear. These precision measurements, more than any fusion ideas in the book, are perhaps Dhalwala and Vij's greatest concession to consumer tastes: while curry, and Indian cuisine in general, has always taken in spices and approaches from neighbouring countries and invading empires while continuing to be strongly regionally defined, precision measurement of spices is genuinely foreign. The novelist Julian Barnes, in his short, comic book of essays, *The Pedant in the Kitchen*, speaks to a longing for specificity that Vij's recipe serves: 'cookbook writers, it seems to me, fail to imagine the time a punter takes holding up a trembling teaspoon and wondering if its piled contents are better described as "rounded" or "heaped"; or glossing the word "surplus" in an instruction like "trim off the surplus fat."' This reminds me that Vij is indeed being consumer-friendly, not Western-friendly – freehanding is part of the game for chefs and food writers across cultures.

Even so, it's telling that imprecision is one of the few true signifiers of authenticity for a dish as inauthentic as curry. The inability to nail down exactly how much of what goes in what is a recurring element of the curry narrative, which Jhumpa Lahiri touches on in 'Rice,' another *New Yorker* essay, this one written in 2009, about her father's mastery of pulao: 'He has a reputation for *andaj* – the Bengali word for "estimate" – accurately gauging quantities that tend to baffle other cooks.' Part of the intergenerational power of the curry metaphor, the idea that something is lost, lies in the dish's very flexibility – while pulao isn't curry, its proportionate measurements are a similarly intuitive affair. In Lahiri's father's case, 'There has never been an unsuccessful batch, yet no batch is ever identical to any other.' Lahiri speaks of how she'd never dare to attempt it, and that's a key part of the ongoing story of meaning-burdened homeland foods: that it has something intrinsically of the maker in it, and perhaps of his or her increased proximity to the nation that originated the dish. That it can't be repeated and is locked in a reality that is purely of the past.

When I first moved out of the house and my mother realized the depths of my incompetence as a cook, she pinned a sheet of paper to the kitchen wall of my apartment (not with a pin, but with a toothpick, running the paper through and affixing it to a pre-existing gouge in the drywall) with recipes for the BASIC MAURITIAN and BASIC INDIAN bases of any number of dishes, featuring onions, garlic, a more-or-less identical meld of spices, and in MAURITIAN's case, ginger. Ginger is almost omnipresent in Indian food, but I'm still surprised for a half second when I run into it in a recipe from Madras or Chennai, due to this piece of paper that is still toothpicked to some area of my brain.

In memories and stories, the diasporic household often becomes a stand-in for the land of origin, a circumscribed set of walls that bound in language, scents, tastes, ethical codes, and patterns of love and communication that start to shimmer and vanish if the front door is left open too long. It's a backdrop to the stories, one encountered so often that I distrust my own household recollections sometimes, as though one of Chitra Banerjee Divakaruni's short stories or a Sri Lankan pal's childhood anecdote has supplanted my memory. But the paper my mother pinned up wasn't a signet of the unreachable past: it was a set of dumbed-down instructions for a boy who had been spoiled nightly at the dining table.

Growing up, I always knew there would be food on the table, in the fridge, a delicious and seemingly inexhaustible supply. Toothpicking the paper to the wall marked a break. For me, the act of cooking was to be about self-sufficiency, adulthood – not a reanimation of childhood. That's what eating is for: manning the pots and pans meant taking the reins of adulthood, a common factor in many immigrant stories and essays – like the one I'm telling now, like Koul's and Lahiri's. But self-sufficiency was the stated purpose of cooking when my mother was making sure I learned how to feed myself — there were no secrets, no arcane codes held back from one generation to the next only to be revealed through hardship, experience, and a moment of deep eye contact signalling admittance to the secrets of our ancient race.

The second curry of note I'll mention is Homecoming Shrimp Curry, which has become the staple meal I associate with Christmas in the Ruthnum household. It's shouldered aside kleftiko and a Persian fish dish with a walnut stuffing as the go-to son-pleaser for my annual returns home, and my parents like it just as much as I do. It's a deep greenish-brown, a shade you don't often see in Indian restaurants outside of perhaps a saag: while Westerners may like brown food, they don't like it to actually be brown. The sauce has a density earned by its ingredients and process: Mom makes the masala with large, motherfuckering onion chunks that would be the star of the dish if the sauce didn't take a midmorning whirl through the food processor before being returned to the pan. The huge shrimp, decanted frozen into a colander from a frozen bag, look like chilled practical effects from a 1980s alien-invasion movie before the sauce catches up to them and they're subsumed into the curry, white and pink peaks in the murky simmer.

Time and varying heat are key to this dish's success, a daylong process of heating, settling, cooling, and boiling whose alchemy seems beyond science. That's often part of curry narratives, too: the ineffable, inexplicable Eastern magic performed on electric Western stoves. Top British chef Heston Blumenthal, on his television show *In Search of Perfection*, where he sought to make perfected versions of classic dishes such as hamburger and steak by seeking out their ur-versions and distilling historically successful processes into a measured, modern method, had scientists do a study on the use of yogourt in the marinade for chicken cooked in a tandoor for his tikka masala episode.

While it was proven that yogourt vastly aided the marinade's absorption, they couldn't figure out why. It just did. While this made for an irresistible TV moment, and I don't doubt Mr. Blumenthal's standards or the BBC's scientist-hiring resources, it strikes me as odd that what seems like a simple matter of chemistry and biology should be insoluble.

There's no magic or formula involved in the time and heat factors of Homecoming Shrimp Curry, but there is particularity. As in many immigrant households, one of my parents prepared food in the morning and reheated it throughout the day, the knobs on the stove and eventually the button on the microwave enduring twists and pokes as mealtimes came around. In the case of this curry, the multiple simmerings are what elevate it to Christmas dinner and my first off-the-plane meal. The basics are simple, and as I can't think of a good reason not to include the recipe, I'll give it to you. Here's a direct paste of the email that Mom sent me so I could botch the making of the dish:

Kay's Madras Prawn Curry

Ingredients:
Large prawns … cleaned and ready
2 large onions … peeled and puréed in the food processor
Coriander leaves washed and chopped up
Tamarind soaked in warm water
Turmeric
Methi … seeds or fresh
Curry leaves … if available
Garlic and ginger about a heaped teaspoonful each
Fish curry powder … (I buy the fish curry powder from Super
    store). You can use the regular or your own mix as well.
    About 3 tablespoons or more … it all depends on the size
    of the onions …

Water or coconut water
2 tomatoes, chopped up
Salt and chilies

Method:
In a large pan heat some olive oil, sauté the prawns with a sprin
        kling of turmeric.
Do not overcook the prawns.
Remove and put aside.
Throw away the liquid.
Heat up some more oil, add the puréed onion … stir till softened
and lightly browned.
Make a pit in the middle, add the curry powder mix (tamarind,
        curry leaves, methi, ginger, and garlic in some warm water).
Add a little bit of olive oil on top and let cook on low heat.
Allow the curry to cook thoroughly with the lid on … but check
        ing often … add a little water or coconut water to prevent
        sticking … then mix the onion with the curry … Now is the
        time to choose the thickness of your sauce … this should
        be a fairly thick one. Add the chopped-up tomatoes.
Let simmer for a few minutes.
Add the prawns.
Simmer some more.
Add your chopped-up coriander and serve with rice or rotis.

I called to inquire about the accuracy of this recipe, and it
turns out my recall was wrong: Mom does food-process the
onions before the cooking starts, not after. The pureeing-of-
the-completed-sauce thing comes, I realize, from a Gordon
Ramsay chicken tikka masala recipe I used to make all the
time when I lived in Montreal, with a roommate who had a
Cuisinart. Mom also leaves out the bit about time lapses and
reheating throughout the day, but that's hard to quantify on
the page. I don't follow the turmeric-fry step of the recipe –

seems to me that the shrimp cook so fast, they should do it in the gravy where they belong. Then again, my dish somehow isn't a patch to Mom's: this is a trope, yes, but it remains true here – I know I can fix it if I master the timing.

There are some moments in this recipe that an Indian-cuisine purist would find harrowing. For example, the 'fish curry powder from Superstore.' At the popular food blog Food52, Bay Area food writer Annada Rathi rails against these concoctions: 'That's when I feel like screaming from the rooftops, "Curry is not Indian!"; "Curry powder is not Indian!"; and "You will not find curry powder in Indian kitchens!"' She's certainly been in more kitchens in India than the zero I've entered, so I'll take her word, but I'll tell you this: every diasporic kitchen I've opened cupboards in contains curry powder, even if it is a home blend of dry spices tipped into an old Patak's screw-on glass jar. Rathi isn't a hardliner – she goes on to note that 'in the course of this article, it has dawned on me that "curry" is the most ambiguous and therefore the most flexible word, a broad term that conveys the idea of cooked, spiced, saucy or dry, vegetable, meat, or vegetable and meat dish in the most appropriate manner available.' The spectacular imprecision of the term speaks to its ability to encompass centuries of food history, cooking, misinterpretation, and reinvention: it's truly the diasporic meal, even when it stays at home. Curry is only definably Indian because India is a country that has the world in it.

There is a truth to the tropes of cooking and homeland and curry, but it can't possibly contain the entire truth: the overlaps in this conversation between writers like Lahiri, Koul, and me are vast, covering our relationships to our parents and a land we barely know compared to the countries where we wake up every day. In the details, the distinct efforts to set personal experience apart – my insistence that Mom has no kitchen secrets and that cooking was never meant to be a key to the exotic but a passage to adulthood, Koul's universal reflections on whether there is a point when one ever stops needing one's mom, Lahiri's foray into cookbook learning – are there, but I wonder if they are present for readers who are drawn to and receive these pieces. Are the brown, diasporic readers looking for commiseration? And are the non-brown ones looking for an exotic, nostalgic tour of a foreigner's unknowable kitchen? The short answer, I believe, is yep.

The introductions to Indian cookbooks often trade on the authenticity of the author's experience and past – their true knowledge of real Indian food – while gently maligning what passes for Indian food in the West. Meena Pathak, who married into the family behind the Patak's brand, started a line of authentic Indian cookery books after being 'amazed by what people in England viewed as Indian food.' The sauces, spices, and pickles that have been produced by Patak's in the U.K. since 1957 are often a touchstone for Indian food that falls short of the authentic mark, though Pathak calls the company a maker of 'authentic Indian snacks and pickles,' perhaps deliberately leaving out the sauce and spice-paste component of the family business.

Patak's produces a lineup ranging from korma to jalfrezi to tikka masala that perfectly reflects the crossover point between the curries that South Asian immigrants to the U.K. popularized in the 1970s and Anglo-Indian cuisine, which arose during the Raj in India as 'Indian cooks gradually altered and simplified their recipes to suit British tastes,' according to Lizzie Collingham. Under British rule, Indians transformed the Mughal dish qurama, initially made with Persian methods described by Collingham as 'first marinating the meat in yogurt mixed with ginger, garlic, onions and spices before simmering it gently in the yogurt sauce. The mixture was thickened with almonds, another Persian trick.' Anyone who's marinated and BBQ'd the non-tandoor cooked version of tandoori chicken will recognize this yogourt bit as a technique that became a mainstay of Indian cuisine. In eighteenth-century Lucknow, as the Mughal Empire declined, dairy was added to many of the dishes that the empire's Indian cooks had been altering for decades, creating a creamy korma that more closely approximated what you'll find in a Patak's jar nowadays. Cooks in the princely Oudh State courts of Lucknow also incorporated further modifications picked up during the Raj years – 'coriander, ginger, and peppercorns which were basic ingredients in a British curry,' writes Collingham. She attributes the innovations in Lucknow to efforts on the part of the Oudh rulers to prove their distinctive value as a cultural capital to rival the Mughal court in Delhi, and food was part of that battle for distinction. The agricultural riches of Oudh and the Lucknavi love for cream shaped the direction of the region's food in the ensuing decades. That the evolution of curry, despite its continuing adoption of spices from around the country and world, exists on a regionally particular time frame is one of the greatest insights to be gleaned from Collingham's detailed history; that the dish has undergone many modifications to suit colonizing tasters is another. Curry's status as a product of empire, adaptation, an absorption of other cultures, doesn't make it any less specific to a certain time or place in Indian history. It just makes it clear that India's past is as inextricable from cultural influence and pushback as the past of curry itself.

Meena Pathak's introduction to her 2004 cookbook, *Flavours of India*, both capitalizes on and reacts against the family's business of U.K.-style curries, by plumbing the past:

> Some of my earliest memories are of going to the market with my grandmother in Bombay (now called Mumbai) and watching her haggle with the vegetable sellers to get the best produce

… In her house, food was always something that was eaten for taste and enjoyment, not just for nourishment …

And here's a complementary, family-nostalgia-heavy passage from the introduction of Australian chef Ragini Dey's 2013 book, *Spice Kitchen*:

My earliest food memories are of the family lunch table, specifically at my grandparents' home, where plates of kababs, curries, sweet seasonal vegetables, crunchy salads, crumbly breads, beautiful rice dishes, perky aachars (pickles) and chutney, softened by velvety raitas, were consumed, while mothers and fathers, aunts and uncles compared their favourite recipes and tips for making the best parathas.

From Meera Sodha's 2015 *Made in India: Recipes from an Indian Family Kitchen*, another paean to the authentic:

I've never lived in India, but I grew up in England eating the same food my ancestors have eaten for hundreds of years and which I still cook in my kitchen, every day.

My family's home cooking is unrecognizable from a lot of the food that is served up in most curry houses across the U.K.; ours is all at once simple, delicious, and fresh. Real Indian home cooking is largely an unknown cuisine …

Shelina Permalloo, a fellow first-generation child of Mauritians (but born in the U.K. and destined to be winner of the 2012 season of *Masterchef*, while I am a Canadian who can cook seven things pretty well), introduces her book with another reach into her family's past, beginning with their family home in Southhampton and ending with a section called 'Mangoes and Memories':

Mum always listens to music while cooking and when I think of the times I used to sit on a little stool in the kitchen being her sous chef, my head fills with memories of old Indian songs and traditional Mauritian Sega songs – classics like 'Bayaboo' and 'Li Tourner' – my mum humming away as she chopped garlic, ginger and onions, the clattering of the rolling pin and the sound of the pressure cooker steaming in the background. Dad would come in and try to dabble with Mum's cooking, but usually he would just pinch the best bits before it hit the table!

The introductory hook of a cookbook, its *raison d'être acheté*, must be an explanation of why the recipes matter. In the case of an Indian cookbook, an authentic experience on the plate can be provided only by the authentic experience of the author. Hence the striking similarity between the passages above, where each cookbook author demonstrates that her recipes are, above all, authentic. You can tell, because each begins with an account of being on the inside, within a family that represents an uncorrupted version of a background and nation that other readers and cooks can't experience, even if they share a parallel family history – these perfected memories of the past promise meals purer than anything a restaurant can dish out.

There's an episode of the reality TV series *Kitchen Nightmares* that I think about a lot, a truth just as embarrassing to write as you think it would be. I call the episode 'Pick-and-Mix,' and watch it on YouTube frequently. I should first flap my hands here and say that it's the earlier, U.K. incarnation of the show, *Ramsay's Kitchen Nightmares*, which was narrated by Ramsay, shot without eighty edits in every conversation, and scored with actual music instead of the splashes and screeches that soundtrack the American version, in which every episode seems to be about a broken family coming to terms with how they can love each other while they clean their filthy walk-in fridge and convince themselves they can clear a million dollars of debt by using the microwave less.

Channel 4's *Ramsay's Kitchen Nightmares*, and this particular episode I'm talking about, Season Five's 'The Curry Lounge,' is full of engineered moments and the occasional sequence of unedited, semi-accidental truth. The premise of the show is that Michelin-starred chef-celeb Gordon shows ailing restaurateurs the way toward financial prosperity and, often, a higher standard of purity in their cooking. The U.K. version lacks the scripted ridiculousness of its American cousin, and this episode's story ends up highlighting a few different models of 'the good immigrant' of the brown U.K. variety, as well as an elegant evasion of the white-saviour narrative. By focusing on telling the brown men in the kitchen that they'll thrive simply by following their home-cooking instincts instead of pandering to white palates, Gordon saves the day through his higher respect for authenticity.

Nottingham, where the Curry Lounge still exists, is a city dense with Indian restaurants and competition. Restaurant owner Arfan Razak, who goes by Raz, is a former pharmaceutical rep whose menu features a 'Create Your Own Curry' option, allowing customers to match their favourite sauce with whatever protein they'd like dredged in it. Ramsay chooses to have a chicken korma with prawns, to prove that the kitchen can't help but make an abomination when the customer is given free reign.

The chef, Zahir Khan, has 'worked in India's best hotels,' as Ramsay's narration tells us. His kitchen brigade consists of 'highly skilled' cooks 'flown in from India.' The food that results from the menu they're given is 'bland' and lacks 'personality,' and in Ramsay's confrontation with the chef and the owner, he makes their problem clear: 'Where that sits connected with Indian, authentic cuisine, it's game over.' The story the dishes are telling Ramsay and the viewer can't be exciting if the eater devises his own meal: part of dining out, particularly in an 'exotic' restaurant, is the delight of ceding control to a connoisseur. Ramsay is as apologetic as his persona allows when he explains to the camera why he has the expertise to correct the authenticity flaws in a restaurant that has little to do with his Scottish upbringing or French culinary education: 'This is a first for me, turning around an Indian restaurant. Now, the basic principles are exactly the same, no matter what the style of cuisine is. But, daunting task. Very excited.'

Ramsay calls the Create Your Own Curry option 'thousands of years of Indian culture straight out the window,' which is noble, but also skips over the adjustments that the British Raj made much more recently and that Gordon would likely still consider authentic, or at least delicious (particularly those generously sauced dishes that Indian cooks devised, according to Collingham, to satisfy the British compulsion to start each meal with a soup course). Gordon pins the blame for the pick-and-mix curry option on boss Raz's desire to please every customer who comes into his restaurant: in the show's story, this is a man who has abandoned the purity of his roots in order to both please and profit from the white masses of Nottingham.

The word *individual* comes up alongside *authentic* as a differentiating factor necessary for any Indian restaurant. With store-bought curry pastes and frozen samosas in the kitchen, the Curry Lounge can't be either, as Ramsay proves by having a tasting in which every dish on the menu is cooked for a blindfold test, and dishes are revealed to be indiscernible from each other. Gordon takes chef Khan to a South Asian grocery and fishes for details on his past, finding out that Khan is from Rajasthan, and his first great culinary influence is his mother's korma: 'Not the korma we make here, the sweet one.' Khan agrees to make his mother's lamb korma as the special that night. 'A new dish you can't get in any run-of-the-mill curry house,' Gordon tells the staff and audience. 'Simple, authentic Indian cuisine.' This dish is the foundational example for the restaurant's future, along with Ramsay's usual *Kitchen Nightmares* tenets of avoiding the microwave, cooking fresh, and so on. This drive to resurrect the authentic, starting in the chef's homeland and zooming in to his own family home, disregards the complicated and culturally mixed history of korma, adapted as it was from a dish brought to the country by the Mughal Empire, the one-time historical combatants of the Rajput rulers.

The remaking of former pharma worker and current Curry Lounge owner Raz as Chef Patron Arfan Razak, Chef Raz, is a fascinating by-product of the *Kitchen Nightmares* appearance. The restaurant's business did turn around, and Raz is one of the few U.K. or U.S. *Kitchen Nightmares* participants who hasn't derided his appearance on the show as a terrible mistake. Though he appears to spend no time in the kitchen in the episode, Raz has since re-envisioned his identity and public image, as a 2012 show reel (likely fishing for further TV appearances) shows.

'We're probably more famous for having Gordon Ramsay in our restaurant,' says Raz, 'but since then, we've moved on in our own right … and one thing I've learned from Gordon and our customers is what we serve in the restaurant is real Indian food, cooked like my mom and my gran and I cook it, in the restaurant, in the home. And that's what I'm really passionate about, is to bring real Indian cooked food to the kitchen table of people at home.'

Raz, whose family is from Pakistan, goes on to demo a tandoori salmon, starting his recipe with a story about his grandmother using her skills as a marinator to disguise fish – which the kids hated – as chicken. He explains that he didn't go to cooking school, and everything he learned in the kitchen was gleaned from his mother, grandmother, and great-grandmother, and a teenaged summer he spent in Pakistan: 'With no electricity, no gas, and relearning how to cook Indian food, or what I call Punjabi food, on a gas stove, and bits of wood.' This incredible melding of terms – Pakistan, Punjabi, Indian – speaks not only to the vastly complicated recent history of the divided north of the subcontinent, but to the difficulty of positioning oneself as authentic in the world of Indian food while still cooking crowd-pleasing classics.

Raz ends his pitch by restating his drive for showing people how to make 'proper food,' and using television to do so, making a transparent bid for entry-level celebrity-chef status. His complete lack of presence as a cook in the original *Kitchen Nightmares* episode is never addressed, nor does he allude to it in any interviews after the fact: the elision of his executive chef Khan from the picture is accomplished through edited cuts of the *Kitchen Nightmares* footage in the show reel.

The authenticity lesson that Chef Raz seems to have gleaned from Gordon Ramsay is not necessarily how to make a restaurant more authentic, but how to make an Indian more authentic. By adopting the narrative of a family spent absorbing cooking lessons from the matrilineal line, by making references to specific places (Pakistan), even if they may not jibe exactly with the place name appended to the food he is making, Raz actualizes his business and his persona as authentic. But the first step, the Ramsay step, was to prove his engagement with the cuisine by positioning himself as the cook, not just the owner. To enter the narrative of curry and authenticity, you have to pick up that wooden spoon.

Raz is an interesting case: his bid to appeal to the masses through his Create Your Own Curry menu is replaced, by his own admission, with a bid to appeal to the masses by proving himself to be the real thing, by showing that his food is the real thing: just how his mother and grandmother and great-grandmother used to make it.

For Indian expats with memories of the country that aren't taken from the remembrances, stories, and writings of others, nostalgia is a different affair than it is for first-gens like Raz and me. Critic, novelist, and creative writing professor Amit Chaudhuri's 2013 memoir *Calcutta: Two Years in the City* is his chronicle of the place where he was born and spent many months during his primarily Bombay-raised youth. He returned to Calcutta to care for his aging parents, and much of the book pits nostalgia based in the carefully maintained artifices of Chaudhuri's Indian youth against the contemporary city where he finds himself. Rooted in his everyday routines as a young man in that superheated metropolis, his particular old-country nostalgia deviates from the majority of novels and cookbooks looking back at India. Really, reading *Calcutta* felt parallel somehow to my infrequent moments of nostalgia for Kelowna, when I feel like driving to the pierogi place where my friends and I had lunch a couple days a week in high school, or remember the attic where we had endless, terrible guitar jams. Chaudhuri's remembrance of Calcutta is specific to himself and to details of the city's past, not the imagined qualities of purity or exoticism so often found in stories (or menus) about homeland nostalgia.

In food terms, the 'continental' dishes at a particular restaurant (including prawn cocktail with coleslaw) are what Chaudhuri thinks of when he summons the Calcutta of his youth. The truth that he looks for in his return to his hometown has something to do with the modern cosmopolitanism of the city he grew up in: what he defines as a 'self-renewing way of seeing, of inhabiting space, of apprehending life.' There's vagueness there, but I get it, especially when Chaudhuri compares his lost Calcutta to the time he spent in unpredictable New York in 1979.

Big, dirty cities and the bad things that happen in them are also closely related to our idea of authenticity. That's part of what small-town kids like me look for in large cities, especially when you grow up a colour other than white in a place that is only white: you want the anonymity that a truly modern place offers. I thought I was vibing with Amit as I read Calcutta, puzzled as I was by his relationship to the city's food: his interest in it is social, historical, but rarely gastronomical. But when he's describing a meal he buys for a poor child, vegetable chow mein, '"chow" as it's called in Calcutta, the commonest, most munificent street food,' he ends his description of the meal with 'I myself have never tasted it.' In a work of reportage, this seems like a betrayal. But *Calcutta* is primarily a memoir, and Chaudhuri's class alienation from the poor and their habits is on full view, as is his carefully maintained distance from tourists, with their roving curiosities for street food that he thinks couldn't possibly be as delicious as we hope it should be. But he never tries it.

That chow mein is a crucial street meal in Calcutta speaks to the crush of cultures and influences that converge in immigrant-rich cities. 'Chinese food has long been Calcutta's favoured foreign cuisine: it belongs to the eternal, and now paradoxically lost, childhood of the Bengali middle class,' writes Chaudhuri. In this city, sweet corn soup, prawn cocktail, and kochuris coexist in urban spaces, perhaps not at the same table, but frequently in one day's worth of snacking. The compressing and absorbing capacities of curry, its ability to borrow Persian techniques, to take up Caribbean chilies and add in fluxing elements to cater to visiting or native tongues, is an acquisitive talent shared by the cities I love to live in and visit. Calcutta, as Chaudhuri describes it, is a city that tastes of its complex history, but is too busy, developing, and cosmopolitan to notice.

Ethnic cookbooks like Mark Bittman's 2005 *The Best Recipes in the World*, and others with similar titles (*Around the World in 450 Recipes, Global Kitchen,* and variations on *A Cook's Tour*), promise access to the different cultures and countries from your own kitchen. Cities hold this same promise: access to the world through eating, as long as you're willing to leg it or pay a few cab fares. In Toronto, I have the option of booking expert tour guide and Sri Lankan émigré Suresh Doss, who drives small groups around the exurban area of Scarborough, where the restaurant selection parallels the ethnic makeup of the people who live and work in the city. Karon Liu, the *Toronto Star*'s food writer, describes the final stop on his tour with Doss: 'There's a place for sushi, East African-Indian, Lebanese pastries, Filipino takeout, kebabs, Chinese and pizza. It's Toronto's multicultural makeup encapsulated in a single-storey plaza with ample parking.' It's a type of access that Chaudhuri, as nostalgic as he is for the dirty cosmopolitanism of Calcutta's past, seems to have little interest in exploring upon his return to the city.

His disinterest in finding urban food experiences that would strike non-Indian readers as the proper kind of authentic is perhaps due to the cheapness of ingredients and domestic labour. Staple dishes are prepared for him at home by servants, for a minuscule portion of his U.K. writing and teaching income. Sujan Mukherjee, a hotel chef, gives Chaudhuri insight into what Calcutta's citizens want from his kitchen: '"People here don't *want* local produce when they come to a five-star hotel," he tells me. "They want something from far away."' Nostalgia for the past doesn't manifest on the restaurant plate for Calcuttan diners, apparently – an authentic Indian eating experience is meant to be had, and go unnoticed, at home.

Chaudhuri's chapter dedicated to food in Calcutta directly addresses curry-relevant cooking only in a section where he describes the lost purity of the cuisine at a Chinese restaurant he'd visited the year before. When a dish he enjoyed is completely changed on his second visit, he summons the chef for an explanation, and gets it:

'Indians not liking those subtle flavours so much. They're saying what is this ice cream, it's not sweet. When American or Chinese visitor come, I making food more Chinese way.'

'Then you should have made it more Chinese way for us,' I said, barely able to contain my frustration.

'I'm not knowing, sir,' he responded wistfully. 'Next time.'

If, indeed, there is a next time. 'Kormaisation' is what this process, integral to Indian cuisine, might well be termed: a suffocation of individual ingredients in the interests of the sauce poured over it, the result of a dozen impossibly unlike condiments brought to a simmer and then turned into this all-purpose national deluge. It's what had happened to the prawns. That chic, suggestive, but eventually vulnerable taste had perished only a year after it had arrived here.

Chaudhuri's aristocratic, even snobby, behaviour in public spaces is jarring to read for someone who's never been part of a certain type of elite: he does acknowledge that the servant/master relationship common between Calcuttan classes is unfair, but says this relationship is only a more personal incarnation of global inequities that he has little control over. His outlook is also singularly colour-blind when it comes to himself and the people he dines with: expecting the chef to distinguish his sophisticated, individual-ingredient-recognizing palate from the mass of Indians who were fans of the 'all-purpose national deluge' of sauce, Chaudhuri seems unaware that when he sits down, he doesn't look Chinese or American. He's just another upper-class brown man who expects a certain brand of perfection for the rupees he's about to lay down.

I'm not sufficiently humourless, nor blind enough to excellent prose, to dismiss Chaudhuri's funny and righteous slam of sauce-rich curries that taste not of any particular spice or ingredient, but of big, dominant flavours: sweet, hot, sour, tangy. It's the signature of a bad Indian restaurant in the West: the sauce is just a different shade of tikka masala sauce, ladled from a row of Subway-like ingredient buckets labelled with a spiciness index. The deliciousness of a particularized foreign cuisine being bowdlerized to suit the Calcuttan palate is an amazing, natural flip of the evolution of curry, and a strong suggestion that 'kormaisation' isn't something that was done only for British eaters. Tastes, and dishes, are meant to change, even in the old country.

Calcutta's lack of stability as a place and a past can be applied across India, as it can across any rapidly changing nation in the West. Life in the old country isn't any more static than it is in the new world, particularly when that old country has been an international hub for centuries, as complex and rich in history as any of its foreign occupiers and current trading partners. Chaudhuri doesn't find the city that he left: any diasporic subject, or first- or second-generation Indian-Westerner, won't find a country arrested in an imagination-flecked past: only a roiling variety of shifting cities, villages, and a country dense with the past and future of a billion people.

Writing about the worldwide outbreak of turmeric lattes in 2016, Food52's Mayukh Sen talks about how he couldn't be angry about this 'hideously awful' drink's co-opting measures, as it is as 'foreign to [him] as it is to Gwyneth Paltrow.' The sheer difference in taste between what's in his mug at Upstate Stock, a café in Brooklyn, and the drink he grew up knowing as milk with *holud*, the Bengali word for turmeric, is so vast that it doesn't register as a theft.

Intriguingly, Sen recounts that the rise of the turmeric latte wasn't tied to a Western yogic stretch for the authentic healthy alternative remedies of India. The 'lifestyle media,' publications ranging from *Elite Daily* to *Bon Appétit*, didn't touch on the fact that stirring turmeric into milk goes back hundreds of years in a certain subcontinental country: it was presented as a tasty, healthy innovation in the hot-drink world. Lifestyle and food writers of Indian origin didn't want to let this pass, presenting a CliffsNotes history of the beverage in several online pieces, with *Mic* deputy food editor Khushbu Shah offering this as a concluding note: 'There's nothing wrong with enjoying something delicious from another culture. The problem grows when credit isn't given where credit's due.'

Sen rightly points to what was missing in this backlash: a sweeping lack of specificity. In these articles explaining the origin of the turmeric latte, this variant on what is called in Hindi *haldi doodh*, '[t]he drink was simply "Indian," a rhetorical device far too generous and nonspecific.' He goes on to talk about the

> limitations of the ways in which we talk about Indian food, like in the manner food that's primarily eaten in northern Indian has become a de facto representative of Indian food writ large. It's a power dynamic bolstered, innocently and accidentally, even by those people who are primed to discuss this drink best: those in India and its diaspora.

The 'power dynamic' Sen refers to here is particularly interesting: it's the Western narrative that has power, I believe he means, and Indian and diasporic writers of Indian origin are backing it up. Diasporic subjects join the discussion promoted by the Western 'we' because they haven't taken note of the minimizing consequences of reducing 'Indian food' to a set of dishes that is Northern Indian. But perhaps the writers of these articles, the ones who claim India as their homeland, are indeed North Indian. The American-restaurant dominance of their dishes may seem a matter of course for them simply because they're not properly versed in the wider cuisine of India.

Or – for the diasporic ones like me, the ones at a farther remove from India than Mayukh Sen, whose parents emigrated from West Bengal – perhaps restaurants shaped their conception of what Indian food is in combination with what was cooked in their homes. The catch-all nature of the term *Indian food* is as non-specific and potentially offensive as Chinese food encompassing Hakka and Szechuan, or Italian food spanning Neapolitan cuisine and Sicilian – but in the diaspora, it does mean something quite specific, just not specific to India. It's what Indian food became out here, in the understanding of the West, a West partially constituted of the products of diaspora, including India's offcuts who ended up in indentured servitude or clerical postings abroad, like my great-great-grandparents in Mauritius. The term *Indian food* may be inaccurate, but it's not tyrannical: it represents a collective, shared brown identity that the products of the diaspora have uneven access to, a collection of modified dishes that touch on shared experience. Just because it's not authentic doesn't mean it's fake: the idea of an encompassing homeland, presented as a recognizable cuisine, can be comforting even if it fails to be accurate or entirely inclusive.

Sen's discussion with Indian cookbook and cooking-show maven Madhur Jaffrey is another wonderfully telling slice of a cross-generational quest for the authentic. Jaffrey, mentioned earlier as Jhumpa Lahiri's textual kitchen instructor in the arts of Indian food, has been a visible face of Indian cookery for the Western home since the mid-sixties. When Jaffrey talks to Sen about Indian food not having yet had its American moment, he replies that he doesn't understand what she can mean, evidenced simply by the incredible proliferation of Indian restaurants, even if most of them do serve specifically North Indian food. Jaffrey clarifies:

She wasn't talking about that Indian food. Little did I know that this woman, six decades my elder and from a completely different part of India than that of my parents, was, in fact, talking about the Indian food I always knew. It's the food that's spiritually similar to what Rinku Bhattacharya writes about in her Spice Chronicles: bhaate-bhaat (quite literally, rice and rice), maacher jhol (fish curry), dishes crafted by hands like my mother's, more hearty and less rich than the ones you'd find in most Indian restaurants.

With 'hands like my mother's,' we are again in the arena of the authentic, with the buried signal that what we're eating in Indian restaurants – though they might be Northern Indian dishes cooked by Northern Indian hands – is not quite real. Sen's clarifications, that he is an advocate of accuracy in writing on Indian food, 'anchored in the specificity of an individual experience without reaching for any greater truths about a monolithic Indian experience,' still don't preclude that 'hands like my mother's' phrase. He's not exactly engaged in a pissing contest for which Indian food is da realest, but he is invested in letting it be known that the food of his parents' state of origin (itself a place of diverse kitchens – his parents make two completely different egg curries) *is* real. The dominance-of-authenticity discourse when we write and talk about curry is such that even unique details – those two egg curries – risk becoming subsumed in the genre's codifications by all but the most perceptive readers.

Finding examples of a disappearing reality tied to the past is a key component of Samanth Subramanian's 2010 book *Following Fish: Travels around the Indian Coast*. This journalistic travelogue is the kind of book that allows you to travel as someone else. The title, self-explanatory as it is, was modified for the book's 2016 reprint, when the subtitle was swapped out for

One Man's Journey into the Food and Culture of the Indian Coast. This is telling for two reasons: one, that the journey is reoriented even more specifically to become a personal one; the reader is being told that there won't just be discoveries of culture and history here, but self-discovery — hopefully of the homecoming sort. And two, with the insertion of *Food* into the title, readers are being assured the book won't be all grim conversations about depleted stocks and the lives of rural fishermen: there will be curries, specific curries, ones that perhaps they've never eaten. Maybe even recipes. Subramanian, a New Delhi/Dublin-based journalist, is in search of a piece of the country that might soon be altered, for traditions and landscapes that may be on the verge of vast change or vanishing.

His quest, as a journalist and historian, parallels Western travelogues from the past century like Gavin Maxwell's *A Reed Shaken by the Wind* or Kenneth Fitze's *Twilight of the Maharajahs*: both books seek to capture what is about to be lost to the encroaching reach of the modern. Subramanian's fascination with the historical circumstances that led to a fishing region converting to Christianity from Hinduism (they needed Portuguese military support to fend off attackers) and the complex relations of fish and spice trading along the coast lead him closer to the authentic than any sense of nostalgia could. The history of India we see here is one of constant interaction and exchange with other countries, the conflicts and compromises that shape a culture and national identity.

There's a chapter in Subramanian's book in which he's cruising Kerala looking for variations on the ideal toddy-shop curry. Toddy is a coconut-palm sap fermentation that pops up in novels about the Raj under the name arrack, but the toddy-shop experience is about as distant from the parasols and cannonballs of those books as one can imagine: these are roadside boozers, where the drinks are served with a meen curry accompanied by kappa. Kappa's made of tapioca, coconut, and chilies, a starch that counters what Subramanian calls the 'over-whelming gravy' of the curry: 'All toddy shop meen curries come furiously red with industrial doses of chilli powder.'

Reading about this dish for pages, I had to attempt it. Subramanian's travelogue contains no recipes, but his regional and lingual specificity makes googling easy. Kurryleaves.com, a detailed, regionalized archive of Indian dishes, had the recipe, and most of what I needed for the rest would be an easy find.

I live in the Parkdale neighbourhood of Toronto, which has the largest concentration of Tibetans in North America. That's part of the reason Indian groceries thrive here, and why vindaloo and bhuna share page space with momos and shap-tak on the menus of Tibetan restaurants: people pick things up in a diaspora, and end up enjoying them, making them, selling them, or some combination of the three. I bought the spice I was missing (asafoetida, used historically by certain Hindus, such as the Kashmiri Brahmins, whose faith-based avoidance of onions and garlic is one of the few truly incom-prehensible culinary quirks I discovered in Lizzie Collingham's curry history). I also picked up two bagged parathas that had been made in the suburbs the day before. I've lost the knack of making rice on the stovetop, thanks to being spoiled by my now-broken rice cooker.

As is true of the slight majority of the meals I've eaten since I moved away from home after high school, I ate the toddy-shop curry alone, going faster as the heat caught up and started to overwhelm me, liquefying everything in my sinuses and then starting to work on my brain. It had that enlivening taste of a great curry, that primal sting of spice and challenge, with enough uniqueness that you seek the space on your carbonizing tongue where a new flavour has landed, as though you could map the regions on your palate and over-lay this with a chart of the country. This intensely regional dish, crammed with spices and techniques picked up and developed in coastal Kerala, came together in my bowl thanks to the vagaries of international immigration and trade that resulted in my neighbourhood grocery stores, long after the ingredients to the general guidelines of the recipe had coalesced (Subramanian notes that there is a range of ingredient differences in the toddy-shop curries). The cycling story of diaspora, of human movement across great spaces, constant dislocation and relocation, is present in mouthfuls of this dish: curry's reassuring power isn't a resurrection of a stable past, but a reminder that the past, and our former countries, are as fractious and adaptable as the present.

Writing about food leads to writing about the complex histories of our relationships to eating, and to food itself. If that food is curry, we enter the metaphysical realm of discussing what's real. Not reality itself, but being *real*. Novels, memoirs, and food writing that touch on authentic experiences of elsewhere, delivered via fork or paratha, enter into a conversation about experience, alienation, authenticity, and belonging: this 'mystical microcosmic' element of South Asian writing plays an important role for both non–South Asian readers and nostalgic brown readers. Eat, pray, love: curry is good for you, especially when it seems *real*.

Readers of 2003's *Monsoon Diary: A Memoir with Recipes*, by Shoba Narayan, can cook along to the author's memories and stories, extending from her first childhood meals in South India to her departure for college and life in America. The dishes lend solidity to the experiences – by cooking along to this book, readers are meant to enter Narayan's journey through the senses. The author recounts the day when her bid for freedom from the family home was cemented: she cooked a feast so convincing that her parents just had to grant her permission to leave. In America, one of her ongoing struggles is persuading her arranged-marriage husband, Ram, that fusion cuisine is an acceptable alternative to the South Indian recipes he's used to.

Monsoon Diary is one of countless books that deal in South Asian food and culture, and extend dinner-table conversation into the discussion of life's greater questions. Narayan examines the particular cards she's been dealt while teaching the reader to prepare a bowl of steaming sambar to accompany her ruminations on fate and belonging. *Monsoon Diary* is an account of childhood, emigration, and diasporic life, and provides consistent links between cooking in the home and keeping a connection to the homeland. Preparing a meal becomes an act of recollection. Even if nostalgia may alter the familial memories that are conjured, the descriptions of food are precise: Narayan's largely unsentimental prose can be strikingly evocative, such as when she describes ghee as 'the vegetarian's caviar.'

Remembering a country in writing – or recreating a country and past that may never have existed – is a form of definition, particularly when the recollection is aimed at an audience. To readers, nations and culture perceived through tales of food and caring family become realms of nostalgia or otherness, defined more by how they are recollected than by their physical existence.

The home, the domestic space, is a crucial part of any immigrant story: it's the place where safety, guilt, and disconnection often meet, and where language is in its greatest state of fusion flux, as Western tongues meld with whatever is spoken in the kitchen. Making a home through food is the constant in Narayan's journey through a past that resulted in a happy emigrated existence in America. A Western audience can read, taste, and visit someone else's past, without having to swap the dice-roll of a love marriage for the dice-roll of an arranged marriage.

Monsoon Diary belongs to that genre I, at first, jokingly, then more thoughtfully, have been calling currybooks. These books, part of the influx of great, good, and bad diasporic literature that came after the early eighties, follow a set of invisible and flexible genre rules. As with all genre fiction, the good ones are good and the bad ones are bad. And if you're a brown writer, it will be presumed to be your default genre, and you'd best recognize that.

In a 1982 essay, Salman Rushdie described several attempts at defining the 'Indo-Anglian' writer, and indeed the idea of Indianness itself, that he encountered at a conference about

Indian writing in the English language. The definitions on offer ranged from a knowledge of Sanskrit to membership in mainstream Indian culture, disregarding the minority cultures of Buddhists, Sikhs, or Muslims. Rushdie, himself a member of that latter group, recollects the point precisely: 'if Muslims were "Mughals," then they were foreign invaders, and Indian Muslim culture was both imperialist and inauthentic. At the time we made light of the jibe, but it stayed with me, pricking at me like a thorn.'

The concept of the 'Indian writer' (especially Indian writers abroad such as Rushdie) has since expanded into the idea of the 'South Asian writer,' the author of 'immigrant fiction': the category has broadened, and the critical need to define brown writers in English by their exact place of physical and linguistic origin has lessened. Contrarily, the critical and popular discussion around what's between the pages of one of their books is perhaps more narrowly definition-focused than ever: as the tropes and genre conventions around books by South Asian authors have accumulated over the decades since Rushdie's essay, the expectations for what brown writers are supposed to do in their work have narrowed.

Hints and swipes aside, what differentiates the kind of work my younger, even more irritating, self began calling currybooks from the greater body of diasporic novels? For one, currybooks typically detail a wrenching sense of being in two worlds at once, torn between the traditions of the East and the liberating, if often unrewarding, freedoms of the West – as with, for example, V. V. Ganeshananthan's 2008 *Love Marriage*, in which the Sri Lankan–American protagonist traces her ancestry and its impact on her present at the deathbed of her Tamil Tiger uncle. There's typically also a generational divide, a bridge littered with pakoras and Reese's Pieces that cannot be crossed except with soulful looks and tangential arguments. Most often we're looking at a displaced South Asian character in the U.K., North America, or Western Europe, searching for place, belonging, and an outer and inner shape to her identity. This protagonist has perhaps been displaced before birth, by her parents.

As South Asian literature (a term just as non-specific but functionally useful as *Indian food*) grew throughout the seventies and eighties to become an increasingly mainstream cultural force in the West, a generic calcification began to appear around certain elements. This thread of diasporic literature became a subgenre unto itself, and it's now a sure thing that you'll find a disconnected-family/roots-rediscovery page-turner with exotic red silks, black braided hair, and perhaps a mango on the cover among the stacked books at Costco, or on a chain-bookstore table under an 'Eastern Journeys' placard. These books bear titles like *The Golden Son* (by Shilpi Somaya Gowda), *The Orphan Keeper* (by Camron Wright, who is white, but the book is 'based on a true story' of kidnapping and orphan-selling in India, and therefore fits comfortably into this authenticity-rich subgenre), *The Hindi-Bindi Club* (Monica Pradhan), and *The Mistress of Spices* (Chitra Banerjee Divakaruni). There is strong, sincere prose in many of these books, while others are solid entertainments. Regardless of literary quality, they typically hit enough nostalgia, authenticity, and exoticism points to score decently on Goodreads.

When these books are really bad, nuance is out the door, as mothers and fathers screech rules and edgy white girlfriends and boyfriends offer drugs. Some of this reflects the lived experience of many South Asians, of course, but the poles of the pure-if-backward East in opposition to the corrupt-but-free West in these stories is drawn so strictly that the books become fairy tales by default. Books that escape the codifications of the genre often interrogate it – Hanif Kureishi's *The Buddha of Suburbia* (later made into a television show scored by David Bowie and starring a pre-*Lost* Naveen Andrews) called bullshit on East and West equally. The protagonist is a sixties hippie teen whose father sets himself up as a junior maharishi in London's suburbs, with unholy goals of sexual and financial enrichment. It's possible for vendors of South Asian spiritual groundedness to make the move west, whether by plane ticket or by book – and it's also possible for South Asian emigrants to the West, and for their children, to long for the truths of the past and a pure homeland.

White writers have certainly pursued the authenticity of the imagined ancestral past that is the birthright of every second- or third-generation member of the South Asian diaspora. Getting back to the real, right thing is, after all, a key part of Elizabeth Gilbert's overwhelmingly successful spiritual self-help/travel memoir, 2006's *Eat, Pray, Love*, a cousin to a certain subgenre of books in the widening field of South Asian literature. Gilbert's travel experience in the book reflects a particularly modern privilege: allocating circumscribed experiences to particular cultures and geographies, designating each place with a desire or goal. In Gilbert's predetermination of how her year of self-discovery was going to unfold, India was the pray-place, after her feasting in Italy. The pounds she gained in experience of gelato, cheese, pasta, and bread on what her friend Susan calls the 'No Carb Left Behind' tour are to be abandoned, along with the spiritual clutter of her past, in her guru's ashram. One of her ashram pals, 'Richard from Texas,' describes the place where Gilbert starts her Indian sojourn as 'a beautiful place of worship, surrounded by grace. Take this time, every minute of it. Let things work themselves out here in India.'

At that line, the quietude of Gilbert's time in India, and its consequent artificiality, becomes striking: in exposing herself to spiritual truth, the overmastering fact of India's population, its crammed density – 'the crowd,' as Salman Rushdie put it in a 1987 essay, 'The Riddle of Midnight,' on the separation of

India and Pakistan – is nowhere to be seen. She's in perpetual peace, with other seekers. From most accounts I've read, extending from the Raj to the present day, peace and quiet in India is an expensive commodity. In the country that Gilbert has allocated the role of finding her inner truth, she's strictly averse to any outer experience. Her resistance to getting out of her Indo-spiritual mode by engaging with the country emerges as a reluctance to taste it:

> A few times a week, Richard and I wander into town and share one small bottle of Thumbs-Up – a radical experience after the purity of vegetarian ashram food – always being careful not to actually touch the bottle with our lips. Richard's rule about traveling in India is a sound one: 'Don't touch anything but yourself.'

This may not be explicitly racist, but it is hilariously cautious – a hundred pages ago, Gilbert was dining on the intestines of a newborn lamb, but in India she'll decide that her needs are best served by staying in the ashram for the full term of her spiritual education. Like Amit Chaudhuri, averse to the street food of Calcutta because it wouldn't dovetail with his idea of a necessary experience of the city, Gilbert has a clear idea of what she's there for. She didn't come to India to eat. Where Italy was a place for gustatory hedonism, India is a place of spiritual honesty and reconstruction, and damned if she's going to allow it to be anything else. Her time in the country, after her days of self-confrontation and looking for the yogic God in herself, ends with a flight out of 'India at four in the morning, which is typical of how India works.' Maybe it is typical – I haven't been, myself. And it's likely that Gilbert has been back and experienced a fuller version of the country since. But can she make the call of what's typical of the country or not after having spent a few weeks meditating in a series of quiet rooms?

Jhumpa Lahiri's experience of Italy, a country she moved to in order to deepen a long-standing relationship with its language, speaks to another aspect of the inescapable realities of travel. *In Other Words* (2015), Lahiri's written-in-Italian account of a mature writer coming to grips with a different language, can't help but become a travelogue, as her Italian can only make the final leap toward fluency by her moving from America to Rome – a trip back to someone else's old country, in pursuit of a language she wanted to make her own.

Despite her advanced level of proficiency in the language, Lahiri's white husband was taken by Italians to be the real native speaker in the family: 'But your husband must be Italian. He speaks perfectly, without any accent,' a saleswoman tells Lahiri, ignoring her husband's clearly Spanish accent and Lahiri's higher level of fluency. The saleswoman can't hear Lahiri's better grasp of the language, simply because she doesn't *look* like her Italian should be better than her white husband's. While Elizabeth Gilbert's Americanness is often called to her attention in Italy, in relation to her body, her manner, and her clunky use of language, the sense of rejection is never as profound as the one Lahiri takes from her experience of her language being deemed inferior to her husband's. Gilbert wanted to visit Italy to eat, to nourish herself in this place-away. Lahiri wants to absorb the country, to inhabit its language and ultimately the place itself. She's confronted with the fact that her racism prevents this from occurring once she leaves the domain of pure language and enters the life of the country: on the Italian pages she writes and reads, she can belong, she can have an authentic experience and be accepted by the language as her mastery of it increases. But in the streets, she's still a brown woman among white Italians. Gilbert's whiteness allows her to shape Italy to fit the preconceived experience she needs to extract; Lahiri can't. To get the Indian experience she needs, Gilbert also has to shut out the country outside and stay in her ashram the whole time – even privilege and whiteness aren't enough to corral the actual life of India on the other side of the meditation gates.

Nothing beats actual travel for a real education, they say ('they' quite often being bartenders or servers or students who spend off-seasons fucking hot Australians or Swedes in hostels and reporting back on markets and forest temples seen along the way). But entering the subjectivity of a novel or a travel memoir is a crucial supplement to a worldly education. Elizabeth Gilbert's India is one I'll never see, because I can as little imagine myself spending weeks in an ashram as I can envision going to astronaut camp or being good at sports. As a minor character says in the film *Total Recall*: 'What is it that is exactly the same about every single vacation you have ever taken? … You! You're the same. No matter where you go, there you are.'

There's a subtle difference between travel and tourism – one deeply bound up with authenticity. Elizabeth Gilbert largely accepts her role as a tourist, as she's shaping each place she visits to the brand of experience she wants to emerge with. Jhumpa Lahiri's sojourn in Rome (where she still lives, writing in Italian) is a purposeful inhabitation of another culture, a visit that's meant to turn into a stay, and maybe one day into a kind of homecoming. Belonging and authenticity aren't quite the same thing, and Lahiri, on account of race, cannot ever completely belong to this other place.

Great travel writing allows you to travel as someone else. And certain brands of writing about food or culture allow you to remember yourself as someone else. Part of the appeal of authentic-Indian cookbooks like *Monsoon Diary* and diasporic narratives like Sabrina Dhawan's script for the Mira Nair film *Monsoon Wedding*, in which members of a dispersed Punjabi family return to Delhi for a wedding and end up confronting past traumas, is the chance to enter someone else's remembering. We want to trace a journey backward, to its completion in the past. The more often a tale of returning to the real in past and homeland is told, however, the greater the chance is that its recurring elements start to ring false. It doesn't help when the publisher's marketing moves, such as inserting *Monsoon* into the title of a memoir-cookbook released a couple of years after Nair's hit movie, transparently commercialize South Asian recollections and nostalgia.

This idea of travelling as someone else drew me to another Italian journey, a fictional one by a contemporary of Rushdie's. In his novel *The Comfort of Strangers*, Ian McEwan talks about the moment of entering the authentic, as his husband-and-wife protagonists enter a space they realize they'd been dreaming of throughout their trip to Venice. Robert, the man who befriends the couple and eventually lures them into an experience so unpleasantly real it involves passing through sex into death, tempts them with the promise of a 'very good place' for food. The place where they end up offers only booze, but even if their stomachs stay empty it nonetheless gives them something they truly crave. It's the real deal, a place where people like them – outsiders – aren't supposed to be.

> Then, despite the absence of food, and helped on by the wine, they began to experience the pleasure, unique to tourists, of making a discovery, finding something real. They relaxed, they settled into the noise and smoke; they in turn asked the serious, intent questions of tourists gratified to be talking at last to an authentic citizen.

This is precisely the same experience-request that books by brown people are often asked to fulfill, and not only for the audience – often, the author also seems to want that experience of becoming an authentic citizen. A trip to the subcontinent is supposed to be more than a holiday, and a book about people of South Asian descent is supposed to be more than a novel. An audience may demand that it fulfill the function of literary tourism, offering not just a glimpse of another place and time, but an experience of authenticity. And for the diasporic writer? He or she gains the experience of that pleasure, *unique to tourists*, of making a discovery, finding something real. The disconnected experience of being a person in the West, let alone a person of colour in the West, doesn't lend itself to a sense of comfort or peace: fitting your own story to a narrative where answers are to be found in a familial, national past can be extremely soothing.

Is there a problem with these expectations existing in the genre? Only that they constrain and limit the potential methods of expression for brown writers. No page can be entirely blank when you have a general idea of the shape of what you're supposed to write. For a diasporic writer, the hidden demand to play both tour guide and tourist could lead to a fulfilling negotiation of identity, family, and place – and it could also seal off other paths of exploration, other stories the writer may feel more driven to tell, to an audience that he or she may suspect doesn't exist. A tacit request from readers to create an authentic experience can, ironically, result in the opposite: false stories, or stories with false elements burying truthful details and experience, built on conventions created by other writers and the categorizations of the publishing industry.

Daniyal Mueenudin, author of the excellent 2009 short story collection *In Other Rooms, Other Wonders*, offers a case study in how the sense of discovering authenticity and the comfort of a homeland can function for readers and writers. The stories are multifaceted and complex, but Mueenudin's introductory essay to the Reading Group Guide at the end of the book drives directly to the authenticity-appeal of his work:

> Half Pakistani and half American, I have spent equal amounts of time in each country, and so, knowing both cultures well

and belonging to both, I equally belong to neither, look at both with an outsider's eyes. These stories are written from the place in between, written to help both me and my reader bridge the gap.

Of the eight stories contained *In Other Rooms*, seven are set in Pakistan and one in Paris. The 'gap,' apparently, is to be bridged in one direction: toward Pakistan, and away from the West. Handily, this journey parallels the biographical fragment Mueenudin provides us with in his essay.

Mueenudin grew up on a Pakistani farm that parallels the parcels of terrain that connect the upper-, middle-, and working-class characters in his stories. He gained insight into the lives of the servants and villagers around his father's property, who paid little attention to him because he was a child: 'I learned the rhythms and details of their lives in a way I never could as a grown-up ... These people, their gestures, and intonations as I observed them in my childhood, appear throughout the stories in *In Other Rooms, Other Wonders.*' After college at Dartmouth in America, Mueenudin returned to take control of the family farm as his father was dying – with the administration of his land stabilized, Mueenudin returned to the U.S., got a Yale law degree, and then a job.

Sitting in my office on the forty-second floor of a black skyscraper in Manhattan, looking out over the East river, I gradually developed confidence in the stories I had lived through during those years on the farm. I realized that I was in a unique position to write these stories for a Western audience – stories about the farm and the old feudal ways, the dissolving feudal order and the new way coming, the sleek businessmen from the cities. I resigned from the law firm, returned to Pakistan, and began writing the stories that make up this book.

Mueenudin's short account of his life is, necessarily, missing details. But it's telling that after being specific about two of his degrees – his undergraduate work at Dartmouth and the law degree at Yale – he skips over his MFA at the University of Arizona, where he began to write the Pakistan-set stories that eventually captured the attention of top NYC agent Bill Clegg. These details are also part of the truth, and parallel the bios of most modern literary writers in the West. Still, for a reading group taking on stories set in a distant land, revelatory of insider truths about many levels of a culture that Mueenudin is in a 'unique position to write ... for a Western audience,' workshop and agent talk isn't salient. In fact, it interferes with the reader's conception of a leap from childhood experience in Pakistan to a not-quite-fulfilling adulthood in the West, then back to studied reflection in Pakistan. What Mueenudin puts across in his short essay is his link to the realness of the Pakistan he grew up in, where he had access to villagers that would be impossible to regain as an adult. He wants to authenticate the stories, by showing readers how he was tapped into a life that was earthy, more about his knowledge of the 'fertilizer, diesel engines, and the qualities of soil' of running his father's farm than the airy irreality of life on the forty-second floor in Manhattan.

To be clear, Mueenudin's pursuit of truths in the past and his half-homeland of Pakistan don't mean he emerges with fanciful or half-baked stories. His hyper-awareness of the unjust but seemingly unchangeable nature of class relations, familial obligations, and the complex inequalities of relationships between the sexes everywhere from Pakistan to Paris make his work much more than a series of souvenir keepsakes of the lives of the unimaginably poor in Pakistan. There is no reason to doubt the sincerity of Mueenudin's deep ties to Pakistan, to dismiss his writing about the country of his childhood as a commercial decision. The stories are enriched by a lack of nostalgic sentimentality about life, rich and poor, in Pakistan, and a tangible discontent and longing for escape that affects characters rich and poor. One of the characters in 'Our Lady of Paris,' encountering his son's white American girlfriend, admits that he wouldn't have minded being born in America: 'The one thing I've missed, I sometimes feel, is the sensation of being absolutely free, to do exactly what I like, to go where I like, to act as I like. I suspect only an American ever feels that. You aren't weighed down by your families, and you aren't weighed down by history.' Mueenudin's connection to his family, his personal history, and its relation to the changing face of Pakistan and to the West point to another reaction to the 'absolute' freedom his character describes. When presented with this freedom, thanks to financial possibility and a top-class law degree, Mueenudin's ties to land and family still have a powerful appeal – one that also attracts readers, both from the West and the brown diaspora, who can't boast his family bonds and lived experiences of a homeland. Books like his don't only give us access to a far-off place by depicting life there with precision: for readers seeking an experience of a different home, closer to the earth than a skyscraper office, writers like Mueenudin provide transport. And there's something about the divided subcontinent that has long made it a place that readers, travellers, and eaters look to for truth.

Even if the subcontinent was never one's home to begin with, it can serve – and has served – as a spiritual home in conversation, books, films, and pilgrimage-like trips. Since the example of the Beatles, a major influx of Western tourists have come to India in search of spiritual reality: the authentic home for the soul that Elizabeth Gilbert sought, a place where truth can be found in spiritual slogans, riddles, in long, cross-legged communions with silence and humidity. Gita Mehta observed both these visitors and the industry of fake fakirs who arose to embrace their curiosity and take their money in her 1979 book *Karma Cola*. As the vivid success of *Eat, Pray, Love* and Chip Wilson's Lululemon empire have proven, the guru era is far from over. It's alive both in the form of useful spiritual relationships and in darker incarnations. There are fraudulent ashrams and cultish inveiglers all over the subcontinent and in the islands where we scattered: everyone has a cousin or six who gives 38 per cent of their income to a Leader who, in exchange, relieves them of their connections to family and friends. In the West, too, gurus proliferate, in small local temples, Sai Baba megastructures, and the Bikram Yoga training camp.

Mehta's book goes beyond simply calling shit on hippies and drawing scolding portraits of false gurus, and many of her observations can be easily drawn over to reflect on the writing and reading of diasporic South Asian lit. *Karma Cola* is history-as-reportage, a sardonic chronicle of minor vengeance for colonialism and yet another rippling development in the relationship between India and the West, the series of colonizers who just wouldn't go away and who the country can now actually extract value from, a welcome variation on the one-way cash flow of the former empirical relationship. India could sell its wisdom, packaged for consumption by America and Europe's young and directionless – or old and directionless, for that matter. A welcome influx of cash in exchange for knowledge or simply the ability to clear one's mind of clutter drifted into post-partition India from Europe and the Americas, and, inevitably, leaked back out – the residual path-to-wisdom promises of the Maharishi giving an often-unwanted sheen of higher truth to the work of writers and cooks who wanted to do good work.

For Westerners, the sixties and seventies represented a key moment in the creation of what Rushdie has called an 'India of the mind.' This India contained simpler, purer ways and answers to the most difficult problems through the miracle of relinquishing worldly wealth to a country willing to accept that wealth. This country-sized temple had been building up in white minds for parts of the past two centuries – George Harrison's sitar lessons just accelerated construction. Mehta writes:

> Earlier in the century the Brahmins of Western intellectual thought had paved the way. Aldous Huxley had struggled with Vedanta and dared to expand his mind. William Butler Yeats … found 'in that East something ancestral in ourselves, something we must bring into the light.' These were the thoughts of the highest caste, the scholar, deliberating on language, meaning and despair.
>
> Now it was the turn of the populists, the Beatles and the Rolling Stones, to become pacemakers for a faltering Western heart, and they achieved a more striking success.

Next in this path of inheritance, decades on from Beatlemania, is the displaced diasporic subject: the brown writer, or the protagonist in that writer's novel, who is embedded in the West but also has a 'faltering heart' in need of revival by the ancestral tonic of a voyage east. Think of Mueenudin's closing paragraph, where he depicts himself adrift in his Manhattan skyscraper, stuck in a job where he knows he simply doesn't belong, before setting off to tell stories of the Pakistan that he knows. Even diasporic writers who aren't writing narratives of nostalgia and healing homecoming must contend with the spectre of creating an India-of-the-mind, both for themselves and for a Western readership.

In 'Imaginary Homelands,' his essential 1982 essay on the plurality of identities possessed by any Indian diasporic writer, Rushdie discusses coming to the dilemma of realism early in the composition of his 1981 novel *Midnight's Children*, and building faulty memories and altered perceptions into his characters to compensate:

> But if we do look back, we must do so with the knowledge – which gives rise to profound uncertainties – that our physical alienation from India almost inevitably means that we will not be capable of reclaiming precisely the thing that was lost; that we will, in short, create fictions, not actual cities or villages, but invisible ones, imaginary homelands, Indias of the mind.

For the past two decades or so, many of the novels dealing with the South Asian diaspora have depicted a solid subcontinent and a wavering West: the mirage is in the writer's and character's present, while the truth lies somewhere in the past, somewhere 'back home.' Chanu, the homecoming-obsessed husband in Monica Ali's 2003 Booker shortlisted, best-selling novel *Brick Lane*, is a prime example of a character who believes his unsatisfying life can only be repaired by reversing his emigration. His lack of a worthy job and appreciation from his superiors in London, his struggles with money and intellectual fulfillment – Chanu believes they'll all be repaired by a return to Bangladesh, while his wife is profoundly skeptical. Ali has the realist sense not to allow Chanu to be proved right, but dozens of novelists influenced by Ali's foundational diasporic novel have accepted the lure of locating resolution and truth in the past. Chanu's return is a disappointment: he goes back to the land of his past, but can't step into an idealized memory, or a younger version of himself. When his wife asks him if the return has granted him what he wanted, he replies, 'The English have a saying: You can't step into the same river twice. Do you know it? Do you know what it means?' Chanu's saying goes further back than the English. It's Greek, Heraclitus, a take on the essential hollowness of nostalgia and the danger of basing decisions around it that's over two thousand years old, and still difficult for readers, writers, and Chanu to actively believe.

Despite Chanu's inability to find a sense of home in the homeland, *Brick Lane* remains striking in its juxtaposition of authenticity-fetishizing techniques and blunt contradictions of fanciful conceptions of the subcontinent. The book opens in Bangladesh, 1967, with a flit through homey squalor:

> An hour and forty-five minutes before Nazneen's life began — began as it would proceed for quite some time, that is to say uncertainly – her mother Rupban felt an iron fist squeeze her belly. Rupban squatted on a low three-legged stool outside the kitchen hut. She was plucking a chicken because Hamid's cousins had arrived from Jessore and there would be a feast. 'Cheepy-cheepy, you are old and stringy,' she said, calling the bird by name as she always did, 'but I would like to eat you, indigestion or no indigestion. And tomorrow I will have only boiled rice, no parathas.'

A couple of lines later, the narrator refers to Rupban's pregnancy this way: 'For seven months she had been ripening, like a mango on a tree.' I'd venture to say that if the writer of these words were white and English, they'd be taken as exoticizing, ham-handed (that self-dialogue, the 'cheepy-cheepy'), the food references sticking out as markers of a situation as recognizably foreign as red soil on Mars.

The designations of poverty, of the exotic, of a cheerful comfort with one's lot, of hospitality and familial closeness over the feast table: it's all there, prefacing the as-yet-unborn protagonist's uprooting to London. Ali herself was born in Bangladesh, which isn't an incidental fact; it lends credence to her grasp of life there. But it's incredible how imagined-from-the-outside the scene seems, if only for how often it has been emulated at varying degrees of qualities by writers after (and before) her.

These currybook elements survive Nazneen's arranged-marriage-facilitated emigration to London: she begins to receive letters from her sister, Hasina, which are presented to the reader in broken English, lacking articles and prepositions. This despite the fact that neither sister knows English at this point in the novel, which means the letters the reader is seeing are translated through Nazneen and Ali – if Nazneen's Bengali dialogues with her husband and friends emerge in plain English, why does this written version of Bengali emerge with such lack of fluency? 'They still playing chess but some of piece are lost there not so many fight now.' These aren't the errors of a native speaker who is bad at writing – they're the errors of a woman writing outside her native language. Nazneen's letters from her sister are doubly translated, first rendered into English from Bengali, and then into broken English, to emphasize the separation between life for women in Bangladesh and the life Nazneen is leading in England. Added to the abject conditions that Hasina endures in her increasingly difficult life, her lack of fluency becomes code for her distance from the relative freedom that Nazneen enjoys in the West, a life she ultimately can't bring herself to abandon when Chanu makes the decision to move the family back.

Hasina's broken-English-Bengali has the same reality as the statues that Nazneen and her husband see in the windows of the Pakistani restaurants near their home:

Days of the Raj restaurant had a new statue in the window: Ganesh seated against a rising sun, his trunk curling playfully on his breast. The Lancer already displayed Radha-Krishna; Popadum went with Saraswati; and Sweet Lassi covered all the options with a black-tongued, evil-eyed Kali and a torpid soapstone Buddha. 'Hindus?' said Nazneen when the trend first started. 'Here?'

Chanu patted his stomach. 'Not Hindus. Marketing. Biggest god of all.' The white people liked to see the gods. 'For authenticity,' said Chanu.

Ali's novel adds a supplement to Chanu's observation: brown readers and writers want to see authenticity, too, especially if it's packaged with a message that the freedoms of the West can be had alongside a long-distance experience of the subcontinent. Ignoring Chanu and Heraclitus, as well as Ali's precise and subtle delineation of the expectations placed on brown writers, the genre that Ali's book flirts with continued to thrive.

In Amulya Malladi's 2003 novel *The Mango Season*, which kicks off every new section with a recipe, tech worker Priya Rao leaves her fiancé, Nick, at the airport to travel back to India after seven years in the U.S. Upon her return, she finds talk of an arranged marriage, yes, but also a vibrant, sensory overload that defines India in the peppier examples of curry-books. 'Everything that had seemed natural just seven years ago seemed unnatural and chaotic compared to what I had been living with in the United States.' Priya retains an American stiffness, and an attentiveness to carefully washing her fruit, as she wards off her mother's attempts to inveigle her into an arranged marriage. Her memories of India, a place she now finds almost surreal, become more authentic, more real, as she reacclimatizes:

'Yes,' I said, and dropped my eyes to my plate where my fingers danced with the rice and the creamy bottle gourd *pappu*. How easy it was to eat with my fingers again. I had forgotten the joys of mixing rice and *pappu* with my fingers. Food just tasted better when eaten with such intimacy.

Throughout her family conflicts and arguments over women's freedom, the sensory largeness of India – the heat, dirt, colours, tastes, and scents of Hyderabad – provides its own unchallengeable argument. 'India was not just a country you visited,' Priya says, in a phone call with her American boyfriend's mother, 'it was a country that sank into your blood and stole a part of you.' Priya goes on describe the smells, tastes, and noise of the country, as well as her hatred of the 'bigotry, the treatment of women,' concluding that it is still her country. Despite this balance of hatred and reluctant acceptance, India provides Priya with a sense of belonging, as well as truths and answers born in the honesty of the conflicts that arose from her homecoming.

In a post-novel appendix in which she discusses the book with the engineering-school classmate whose name she borrowed for her main character, Malladi talks about how using India as a setting for her protagonist's epiphany allowed her to use reality, to avoiding having to 'make up stuff': 'For me writing *The Mango Season* was like taking a trip to India. I'd forgotten how good chaat tastes, or how good ganna juice tastes and when I was writing about it I could all but smell that sugarcane juice.' Malladi's recreated India, then, isn't an India of the mind, to her: it's a recreation of the place, the novel itself a comfortable return to the country she left. Her descriptions of food do ring true, and I want to taste that sugarcane juice, too. The very casualness of Priya's quick passing over of caste and class issues in phrases such as her aside about how the 'maidservant Rajni was not a Brahmin and so she was not allowed inside the kitchen' serve as a jarring reminder that India is, indeed, a different place. The abrupt and frequently hammy dialogue, however, along with Priya's sweeping pronouncements about the country's narrow-mindedness, do give readers, or at least this reader, pause. Is this India that Priya returns to, and that Malladi re-inhabits on her novelist's 'trip to India,' being viewed with heightened clarity after years away, or with a new collection of Westernized views? Despite Priya's respect for the 'essence' of India, for its changeless place as her country, she discovers that the country

> was not home anymore. Home was in San Francisco with Nick. Home was Whole Foods grocery store and fast food at KFC. Home was Pier 1 and Wal-Mart. Home was 7-Eleven and Star-bucks. Home was familiar, Hyderabad was a stranger; India was as alien, exasperating, and sometimes exotic to me as it would be to a foreigner.

Yet even a negative nostalgia, the state in which Priya has arrested India as the repository of the family, prejudices, arranged marriages, and provincial values that she was desperate to escape as a teenager, provides the answer she needs: the place she is from, her country, is a fixed part of her past, unchanging and behind her. The truth she takes with her is that her present and future can happen only in the West.

Malladi's titular mangoes have a symbolic weight equal to my beloved curry, especially to the marketing departments of publishers. Pakistani-American novelist Soniah Kamal ran into a mango dilemma that she describes in her 2016 essay 'When My Authentic Is Your Exotic,' wondering whether including the fruit in her book would become a statement:

> If I put the mango in, was I a sell-out? If I took it out, was I being true to the season? What fruit could I substitute? A jamun? But what is the English name for jamun? Should an English name even matter, a jamun being a jamun, like a corn dog is a corn dog. Would I yet have to italicize jamun? Who is the audience for my novel, anyway? Everyone? But what does everyone mean? Should I stick to an apple or a banana? Or would that be too generic?

Finally deciding she 'can neither deny reality for fear of the disdainful Eastern eye any more than I can write in fear of needing to fulfill the expectations of the orientalist Western gaze,' Kamal allowed her characters to eat the goddamn mangoes, which made perfect sense in the scene she was writing, set at the peak of Pakistani summer. Reading this essay, I knew that the mangobooks Kamal dreaded seeing her novel shelved amongst were my currybooks – books that signal their falseness by underlining their authenticity, and placing that authenticity in a homeland lost to time and distance. The blended, diasporic person, existing away, is torn from one place, yes, and exists in another place, yes: but to assume that the before-place, the India or the Mauritius or the Trinidad, possesses a heightened reality and truth, what Kamal calls 'the authentic exotic'? That's not something I can accept in what I read, write, or remember. It's also a type of narrative that does injustice to the true complexity, hilarity, danger, and weirdness of life as a brown person living anywhere in the world, either far away from their supposed home or right where their ancestors have dwelt for centuries.

Kamal passes over another audience, neither the 'disdainful Eastern eye' nor the 'orientalist Western gaze' that she never wants to write for. It's the diasporic reader, a first- or second- or third-generation-away-from-the-homeland person who also longs for a version of what Malladi serves in *The Mango Season*. Western isn't actually synonymous with 'white' – we live here, too. The diasporic sense of nostalgia, of belonging, of home, isn't simply shaped within brown households. The West leaks over the threshold, creating an overlap in what diasporic and other Western readers want from books by brown writers: and in that overlap is authenticity, and a sense that there is solidity, reality, and truth in that place and past that was left behind.

While the growth of the South Asian genre hasn't injured the capacity of diasporic and subcontinental writers to produce original, unique works, genre rules and parameters emerged as the commercial viability of immigrant fiction became clear, and editors and publishing boards began to seek variations on a certain type of brown story. There's profit to be made in a relatable, seemingly authentic presentation of race and culture, even if there's a placeless tinge of Westernization, subtle and ignorable under a formulaic blend as precisely calibrated as a Marks & Spencer chicken tikka masala. (I haven't had one of these since M&S closed their Canadian stores in the nineties, when I would occasionally nuke one of them for a treat – if my preteen palate can be trusted, they were at least as rich as the real thing, even if something was missing in the flavour, and certainly from the soft fibres of the defrosted, industrial chicken). But what's lost in this pursuit of the authentic is, perhaps, the reality of what lies in that placeless tinge: differentiated immigrant existences, ways of being and tasting that aren't about pursuing the lost, truthful flavours of generations past.

Is there something wrong with finding comfort and truth in tropes, whether as a South Asian writer or reader? Kamal and most other brown writers, including me, dread the idea of 'serving' a white audience, which is what tropes most clearly signal to people trying to publish in a market dominated by white editors and readers. In her essay 'Why Am I Brown? South Asian Fiction and Pandering to Western Audiences,' Jabeen Akhtar describes the defining elements of pandering 'South Asian novels published in the West from 2000 forwards,' an era she sees as having been 'ushered forth by [Jhumpa Lahiri's 1999] Pulitzer Prize–winning *Interpreter of Maladies* and all the copycats that followed.' Tagging her list onto the end of writer Jeet Thayil's exhaustion with the 'mangoes, spices and monsoons' that define these books, Akhtar adds 'saris, bangles, oppressive husbands/fathers, arranged marriages, grains of rice, jasmine, virgins, and a tacky, overproduced Bollywood dance of rejection and obsession with Western Culture.' Akhtar is also the author of 'The 17 Elements of a (Bad) South Asian Novel,' which I'm pretty sure is the essay that made Sandip Roy realize that his 2015 novel, *Don't Let Him Know*, was slightly trope-ridden.

'There was a recent article that had come out,' Roy explained in a radio interview with NPR, 'which talked about all the familiar tropes of South Asian fiction in America, and they had mentioned in there – mangoes, arranged marriage, a wise grandmother. And I went through the list and I was like, oh, my god, I have all of them in my book … But I'd like to think that I have them for a reason. I have them because they came naturally to me, and it was lovely.' Here's how the tropes that Roy is referring to shake out in one part of *Don't Let Him Know*, where a character tells his mother that he intends to follow through on his dream of becoming a chef:

'But you never even stepped into the kitchen when you were a boy in Calcutta,' she said. 'What do you even know of cooking?'

'I'd love to cook, Ma, if only you'd let me step into the kitchen,' he said sharply. 'Ever since you came you've just taken it over. I've learned to cook in America and I really enjoy it.'

'You do?' She stared at him as if here was a stranger. Chefs were perfectly coiffed celebrities like Madhur Jaffrey in beautiful silk saris, not Amit. She couldn't imagine him on television with an apron around him talking about sautéing chicken breasts and marinating kebabs.

'It's like meditation,' he said. 'It calms me.' Then he paused and said, 'And maybe you can teach me how. I could watch you and maybe we'll even recreate your recipes, write a cookbook together – "Bengali Meals for an American Kitchen." Wouldn't that be fun, just you and me?'

Romola smiled and shook her head gently at herself. She had been afraid she had lost Amit to America. Who could have thought that accursed letter from so long ago would bring him back to her? They used to call him her little tail when he was a toddler because he'd follow her everywhere. Today he was looking at her with those same eyes again as if she knew the answers and could wrap him in the love of her sari.

The stories that come before us are inescapable. When Sandip Roy talks about how tropes came 'naturally' to him, it's not just that the tropes reflect real circumstances of his background and life: it's that the books and stories that came before him have embedded genre rules that can only be evaded by a determined writer.

But as Kamal points out, mangoes really do grow on the subcontinent. So do the spices, even if they were imported some centuries ago. Perhaps there's a native truth to genre conventions that catch on so solidly – Sandip Roy may say so, in defending the tropes in his novel that reflect his own experience. Just as the heroic beats of action cinema and the trials-to-consolations rhythms of romantic comedies resonate with audiences and creators, immigrant novels that cleave to embedded beats of authenticity still speak of a genuine sense of displacement that, while it isn't always based in lived experience or doesn't always hearken to a past and other place that actually exists, appeals to a vast range of writers, readers, and watchers. They – we – are in need of confirmation that the alienation we feel is at least shared, that it resonates for another, and that there is perhaps an answer to it in an embrace with the realness of another place and culture, the one that was truly always our own.

Immigrant narratives allow readers to live in someone else's past while sharing their sense of the fragility of that particular history: that the sense of alienation has roots in reality is as important to the reader and the writer as the idea of a distant land and a time that holds answers. For the brown-skinned writer, some versions of nostalgic existence are more appealing than others. 'The ideal fusion fantasy,' observes Githa Hariharan in *Almost Home*, 'is a global address that allows you to hold on to the safe familiarity of provincialism.'

In both the writing and the living, the deeper into detail you go – as is true for any place, people, or culture – the more a narrative of collective mass culture becomes a story of particularity, of regional and familial specificities, often defined against the stories outside of themselves. The diasporic bond is a shared, invented history, based on real events and a real place, but shared only as a tissue of agreements, disagreements, and ideas imposed from the outside. Cultural and family history is a fruit that expands as it is peeled, until it is too large to be gripped in the hands or the mind.

I can't remember what books I brought with me to Mauritius, but I do remember one my father gave me while we were there. It was a yellow hardcover storybook, *The Panchatantra*, full of superb and cruel Indian animal fairy tales. In one story, an annoying bird explains to a monkey that the food he's trying to fish out is part of a trap that will snap shut and kill him if he gets to it. The monkey throws the bird against a tree, killing it, then grabs the food, discharges the trap, and is crushed to death. The last line is 'And that is the way of the world.'

Even as a nine-year-old, I appreciated the lack of sentiment. It hinted at something missing from the shining distortions of Grimm's stories I'd encountered thus far, and seemed to suggest that the place where my skin came from was a place where people talked straight, a quality I aspired to possess.

Another memory from that trip: the entire country seemed to treat street traffic the way high school kids treat hallway movement. And I was genuinely surprised by how I was read on the streets – I asked my father, about a week in, why market vendors addressed me in English directly, why they tried to sell me souvenirs instead of groceries. 'It's … the way you walk,' he replied, sparing himself a longer discussion while I dealt with this riddling proposition. Was it possible that I had a distinctive, Western walk – not a John Wayne swagger, but a sort of financially comfortable mince that broadcast my foreignness? Did I walk white?

With my family, I'd already visited Vancouver and London, and in those cities, I knew I could exist the way I wanted to, unnoticed and anonymous in an urban mass of skin and clothing so uniformly varied that individual distinctions became important only if you were looking through the crowd for someone you already knew. There, I'd blend right in. Despite the options on offer in these metropolises, we ate in Indian restaurants on every vacation. The food wasn't like what my parents made at home – cream, butter, and ghee were absent from the version of Mauritian home-cooking I grew up with. But these vacation meals must have been nostalgic reminders to my parents of their student days, when those U.K. Indian restaurants boomed and Mom and Dad were out of their own parents' homes for the first time. Dad sharpened his cooking skills in the residence hall of his Glasgow medical school, but Mom already knew her way around the kitchen, having learned to cook for her fifteen siblings before getting into nursing school and sending back money to provide for them in a different way. The Indian restaurants of Glasgow, and the formulations that the probably-Bangladeshi chefs were coming up with, weren't a taste of home for them, but part of the new exotic of the world beyond their island: these creamy, meat-filled curries that had nothing to do with their family dinner tables, beyond garlic, ginger, some chili, and cumin.

Mauritian food is different, just as Mauritius is different from India, even if I constantly conflate the two in conversation, and also in this book, to avoid the multiply-hyphenated descriptors that pure accuracy would demand. The early history of the island is what teenage me would call a 'colonial gangbang' any time a half-interested friend inquired. A small dot off the coast of Madagascar, Mauritius was one of those barren islands that was in fact verdant and teeming with jungle and diverse species, including the dodo, lying fallow for colonizing powers – pretty much all of them – to settle and make farms, staffed first with slaves, then indentured servants, depending on the barbarism of the empire and the time. The Dutch, then the French, then finally the English took it, with the Portuguese making a couple of disinterested visits sometime in the sixteenth century, when they were already nicely set up in Goa and Ceylon. The British Empire 'won' Mauritius in the Napoleonic Wars, carving out space for the island in Patrick

O'Brian's *The Mauritius Command*, perhaps the only international bestseller with my ancestral home's name in the title.

Aside from that one visit, I know the place through stories, sketchy histories, and folk tales. But I can't dress it in longing that I've never felt. The nostalgia that my parents feel for it, that they impart in their recounted memories, is one that anchors it as the past, not as a place of future revelation or truth for me. The language there, officially, is English, but it's Creole and French that seem to come at you most on the streets. The 1.3 million people who live there are a true mix: 25 per cent are Black and mixed-race people primarily of Madagascan or Mozambican origin, many of whom are the descendants of the slaves brought over by the Dutch and French. When the British assumed rule and abolished slavery in 1835, the Indians who now make up about 70 per cent of the population arrived, mostly as indentured servants. Amitav Ghosh wrote of this exporting of coolies in a trilogy of historical novels – *Sea of Poppies*, *River of Smoke*, and *Flood of Fire* – that I'll get around to reading someday. Descendants of the French and British elite still live there, along with about 30,000 people of Chinese descent, Hakka and otherwise.

Somewhere in that influx of people in the late nineteenth century, with Indian servants in demand to fill labour and administrative roles after outright slavery had been outlawed, my ancestors arrived in Mauritius. The Colonial Office List for 1886 lists a V. Ruthnum as a clerk in the Stipendiary Magistracy at Black River in Mauritius (the British name didn't stick – it continues to be called Rivière Noire on maps and in conversation). It was perhaps this V. who made the first diasporic step out from India, joining what I might fancifully envision as a Wild West trial run for the melting-pot urbanity I'd come to depend on as an adult. Except, in V.'s case, there was no escaping his place in the chain of subjugation where he was somewhere in the lower middle and a white man was at the top.

There's certainly a currybook to be written about V.'s journey, but the happy ending doesn't come until a few generations after his death.

Alienation and a sense of being severed from the past is visited on South Asians from the outside on a daily basis, in forms ranging from violent racial attacks to the ongoing, often lightly intended and genuinely curious 'Where are you from?' that isn't asking where you grew up, but where you were supposed to grow up if your parents hadn't up and left. Alienation has branches, and the thickest and most poisonous stalk of alienation in the West is fuelled by racism and the norm of whiteness. The actor Kal Penn, who played the protagonist in the film adaptation of Lahiri's *The Namesake*, as well as my beloved Kumar in *Harold & Kumar Go to White Castle*, touched on this brand of alienation when he was interviewed with his *White Castle* co-star John Cho by the *Chicago Tribune* in 2005:

> 'Along those lines, I was probably in 4th grade when *Indiana Jones and the Temple of Doom* came out,' Penn says. 'There were all these Indian characters that were eating monkey brains and snakes for dinner, and doing all these things that had absolutely nothing to do with being Indian at all. I went into school, and with myself and every other Indian kid I know, nobody would sit next to us at lunch, for months, because they were convinced we had monkey brains in our sandwich. Those are the media images that go into people's heads. If you don't have close friends to disprove that – or even if you do but you're only in 4th grade – that's pretty powerful.'
>
> 'That's my favorite movie,' Cho deadpans.
>
> Penn sighs dramatically. 'I hate you.'

Penn's story, and many scenes in *Harold & Kumar*, capture the alienating effects of casual racism, whether malicious or ignorance-based, but his sweep of 'every other Indian kid I know' leaves out another form of exclusion that South Asians dole out and suffer from, not least of which because we've been rounded up under this loosely applicable term that covers all the differing cultures and countries of our manifold backgrounds. As Rushdie pointed out in 1982, 'This word "Indian" is getting to be a pretty scattered concept.' On my first day of high school, one of the older Sikh boys signalled me over at lunch and asked, 'Hey, you speak Punjab?' When I said no, he smiled, and the conversation was over.

My Mauritianness, as touristy as it struck the actual Mauritians, was also false currency when it came to recognition by brown kids of a more direct Indian origin, ones who had a closer relation to specific regions, religions, social strata, and experiences that make up that massive and complex country. Being second-gen made me counterfeit Mauritian back in my old country, and I continued to ring false to South Asians who were more closely aligned with India, Pakistan, Bangladesh – the core that we scattered from. The ways to not-belong as a brown teenager in white, small-town Canada are even more complex than my Beavis haircut and Black Sabbath T-shirt could express in 1996. If *Indian* is a baggy term, *South Asian* is parachute pants.

In the 2016 book *Brown: What Being Brown in the World Today Means (to Everyone)*, which blends memoir with focused reportage, author Kamal Al-Solaylee speaks of brownness as 'a continuum, a grouping – a metaphor, even – for the millions of darker-skinned people who, in broad historical terms, have missed out on the economic and political gains of the post-industrial world and are now clamouring for their fair share of social mobility, equality, and freedom.' Al-Solaylee sees brownness as a 'burden' carried everywhere we go: 'Pretending that it's otherwise is intellectual dishonesty.'

Al-Solaylee's intensively researched and reported book is a doors-open investigation, conducted in quite the opposite manner to the table-bound text-and-meal interrogation you're reading right now. Al-Solaylee seeks out the particularities of brown experience all over the world, from Sri Lanka to Hong Kong to Qatar to Toronto. And yet, he begins and emerges with a sense of a united brown identity, even if it is one initially imposed by an outside gaze:

> For much of our history, we've been defined by others – as the brown race, as the weaker tribe, as the civilization-ready subjects of empires. But the time has come for us to self-identify as we wish. There's strength in numbers and comfort in knowing that one's experience is not isolated or an aberration. Whenever I get pulled aside when crossing the U.S. border, I find it reassuring that I'm not the only brown face. I see the Iraqi or Pakistani business traveller, the Colombian student, the Sri Lankan chef or the Indian family with three or four or five children, and I know that while our stories are different, we find ourselves singled out because of our brown skins and histories.

Al-Solaylee's version of self-identification isn't a call for a flattening and universalizing of brown experience to create one narrative of what it is to be brown. As his detailed exploration of regional and class differences in the experience and perception of brownness across the world proves, his is a nuanced vision of a collective experience. As a different sort of storyteller – not a journalist, but a fictional inventor – I buck slightly against even this multi-faceted take on what we share as brown people. Perhaps, and this is certainly born of coming from an upper-middle-class background and living in urban centres, I don't want to self-define as part of a brown identity that is still shaped by outside perception, by the imagination that the majority imposes upon us. The realities of racism and the white majority dominance of life in the West defines how brown people are seen, how they must act, and what they are allowed to achieve – but this doesn't need to limit our imagination of ourselves, or lessen the distinctness and individual nature of experience, especially as expressed in art, in memoir. As brown people in the West, our stories don't have to explain ourselves to white people, or to each other – they don't have to explain shit. They don't even have to suggest that brown people *are* a we, or a they.

Harold & Kumar Go to White Castle came out in 2004, four years after I'd already moved to Vancouver, four years after it could have done me some real good, in high school. Rewatching the movie now, I can see how the casual objectification of the invariably hot female characters clutters the movie's efforts to humanize the Asian and South Asian protagonists. *H&K* is a stoner movie, in direct genre lineage from movies like *Half-Baked* and the *Cheech & Chong* series, but it also has much in common with college sex comedies like *Revenge of the Nerds*, many of which had painfully stereotypical depictions of gay and non-white characters to accompany rampant, dehumanizing misogyny. *Harold & Kumar* corrects the racial elements, even if the depiction of women as sex objects remains in line with long-standing genre conventions. Co-writers Jon Hurwitz and Hayden Schlossberg started by writing their protagonists as young American guys.

'We always had a very multicultural group of friends,' Hurwitz told the *New York Times* in 2008. 'One thing that struck us was that no matter our ethnic background, we were very much alike. But whenever we saw Asian or Indian characters onscreen, they were nothing like our friends, so we thought we would write characters like them.'

I was deep into cinema when *Harold & Kumar* came out, arguing about Antonioni's lack of merit and making a case for Bergman's *Winter Light* as being a more truthful re-envisioning of the director's own *The Virgin Spring* – but it was *Harold & Kumar Go to White Castle* that had a marked effect on my 2004.

The movie's excellent performance on DVD after failing at the box office, and the fact that it was about stoners and goofy shit before it was about race and belonging, made it an incredible sneak attack of a film. Kal Penn as Kumar, who has all the mental equipment and skill needed to get into medical school but doesn't want to fall into an Indian-American stereotype profession just to please his father, gave people around me, especially when I spent part of that summer in Kelowna, the equipment to actually perceive me. It was my first true experience of representation mattering, because it was the first time I felt my brand of the brown diasporic experience had been accurately represented onscreen. In a fucking stoner movie, of all things. Instead of being looked at as an E.T.-like curiosity by white people, Kal Penn is a legitimately attractive possibility for women, as is John Cho's Harold – this made a real difference in non-cosmopolitan places, where coloured skin was an aberration in the yearbook. By aligning itself with so many of the standards of stoner films and college sex comedies, *Harold & Kumar* subverted the genre with the elements it flipped: colour and culture, making the ethnic leading men into a pair of American dudes who did indeed confront racism and address their thoughts on cultural pressures, but only along the way as they sought to get burgers, find meaning in life and work, and yes, to get laid. Ejecting the traditional immigrant narrative was what made *H&K* an important movie: it was allowed to be a dumb, clever look at smart and funny dudes whose cultural origin wasn't the most prominent aspect of their thoughts and lives. The recent *Master of None*, Aziz Ansari and Alan Yang's Netflix series about an immature Indian-American and Taiwanese-American best-pal duo in New York, owes something to *Harold & Kumar* – namely, this foregrounding of non-racialized aspects of the two main characters, even as Dev's and Brian's stories often do feature short dives into the past and their heritage via their parents. (Incidentally, Ansari tweeted that he and real-life friend Yang have been frequently mistaken for Harold and Kumar on the street.)

Brown people, especially young ones, are expected to have an opinion on Aziz Ansari and Mindy Kaling. When I tell people I love comedy, I know that three questions in I'm going to be asked how much I love Aziz and what I think of *Master of None*. Actually, I harbour some resistance to even watching that series and *The Mindy Project*, if only because I know I'm supposed to. It's bizarre to have an expectation of watching a sitcom and forming an opinion about it placed on you, but as a brown person who thinks and writes about culture, that's the deal: there isn't much diasporic comedy on North American television, so it's only fair that you turn up and take it in.

Perhaps Aziz doesn't much want to be the mouthpiece of a brown generation, and Kaling may be equally disinterested. I know I don't enjoy the general expectation that I'm a fan of either, or that I should have a stance on exactly how they let down the depiction of what brown life in the West is *really* like. Ansari, writing in the *New York Times*, points to a different truth: that representation, full stop, matters a lot to people of colour in the West, a fact he's carried with him as he wields increasing control over casting his own show and appearing in work by others. Growing up in South Carolina, Ansari 'rarely saw any Indians on TV or film, except for brief appearances as a cabdriver or a convenience store worker literally servicing white characters who were off to more interesting adventures.' *Master of None* has been part of changing that filmed reality: Ansari and Yang gave us South Asian and Asian leads who had fuck-up careers, dated girls, did the *Seinfeld* and *Larry Sanders* stuff that had long been white territory. Ansari, who plays, in the show's first season, a constantly auditioning actor, has his character lose out on parts due to his unwillingness to do Indian accents. Both Dev in the show and Aziz the creator are staking out space for brown people in the West who don't conform to the familiar Apu Nahasapeemapetilon take. It matters to see our first-gen and second-gen bodies and Western lives reflected in some form on the screen, by writers of comparable origin – of course it does – but what matters even more is that every mass-culture take on Western brownness from a brown voice isn't given credence as the defining take, or the one that all succeeding texts, shows, or movies act in response to or in imitation of.

Even if it is a counterstream take like *Master*, there's a genuine sense of despair when you see one story of Western brownness upheld by whites and members of the brown audience alike as the one that seems true: a sense that what you have to say or write may only be relevant in relation to the story they've seen or read before. That you're either carrying on the same narrative or reacting against it and, either way, that original story is the one that matters.

And the movies and stories that don't subvert the conventions of an immigrant narrative? They can still resonate. Hacks like Dan Nainan, the fifty-something comedian who poses as a millennial and groomed an intricate fake connection to internationally successful stand-up Russell Peters in order to snag high-paying gigs at Indian-American weddings, use their South Asian heritage as the basis for massive swaths of their material, relying on recognized commonalities instead of crafted jokes for laughs. And often (though not in Nainan's case, as his act is just too terrible), those laughs happen. Diasporic audiences often crave confirmation that the alienation we feel individually is shared, that it resonates for others. In currybooks, an answer to that alienation is floated: embracing, even if only within the span of a few hundred pages, the realness of another place and culture, the one that was truly always our own.

Still, shouldn't approaching pain, alienation, displacement, and a sense of cultural unbelonging come from a place of incomprehension, not a predetermined inquiry that holds that the

East has answers to the dissatisfactions of a life in the West? I'm not telling you, I'm asking. But it's a pointed ask. Does Saroo, protagonist of 2016 Best Picture nominee *Lion*, based on the true story of Saroo Brierley's incredible discovery of his village roots after being lost and raised by an Australian family, truly resolve core questions of his existence when he learns that he's been mispronouncing his own name for his whole life? And what does his discovery do for us, for the audience?

It tells us that there's an answer, a true and calming reality, in the embrace of the past. As a character – I won't presume to speak for Saroo Brierly, co-author of the memoir *Lion* is based on – Saroo's real name will likely always be the mangled mispronunciation of his authentic name, a variance on *sher*, the Hindi word for the film's titular *Lion*. His immigrant existence is a mixed, complicated, in-between one, a balance formed by turmoil and forward motion, not the peace of answers found in the past. The popularity of these narratives, and the relationships that diasporic writers have with them as both authors and readers, are part of another tangled story we tell each other and ourselves, wondering ultimately if they are something that white Westerners are interested in for reasons that would make us uncomfortable.

Distance from questions like that is what I once wanted from travel, and now require of the cities where I choose to live. A society in which one's movements and appearance are met with utter indifference is my ideal, one that comes closest to being incarnated – for people of South Asian descent, at least – in cosmopolitan cities. On that trip to Mauritius, seeing key chains and tubes of sand from Chamarel extended to me in automatic recognition that I was a tourist did feel like a kind of homecoming: a recognition that I wasn't any more at home in that country than I was in small-town British Columbia. In B.C., my race differentiated me – in Mauritius, it didn't help me to fit in. I bought both the key chain and the tube of sand and showed them off to my friends when I got back.

It's more than just a white audience wanting to hear our real experiences: it's us, the diasporic audience, wanting to read experience reflected back, or to see a familiar version of a story. Fariha Róisín, writing on *Bend It Like Beckham* in the online cultural magazine *Hazlitt*, uses a collective 'we' in discussing South Asian identity while she points to some of the isolating historical wedges within the great mass of Western brownness, particularly the 'realities' of children being expected to follow cultural expectations enforced by the families:

> ... our language for who we are as South Asians in the West is still so young, still so undefined. We have so much internalized hatred amongst us; the running joke in *Bend It Like Beckham* is that Jess can marry anyone, just not a Muslim. We've refused to detail our shameful and horrific interlacing pasts. That the current Prime Minister of India, Narendra Modi, has been accused of participating in a cleansing of Gujrati Muslims in 2002. Or that my very own Bengali parents survived a Civil War, where three million majority Muslim Bengalis were killed by the Pakistani Army in 1971. Or that Pakistani Muslims killed Sikhs in Punjab in the '40s, and vice versa. Or that Kashmir is still a tentative region over a debate of religion and ownership. We don't give voice to the hatred we have for each other, and therefore we are unable to unpack the absurdity of it, when in so many ways our histories are richer, intensified, and made more glorious because of what we've shared through the ages.

Perhaps war is essentially absurd, and certainly conflict is inevitable among the various culturally and religiously diverse people assembled in one area of land over centuries, particularly when that land is colonized and partitioned – but calling a history of conflict between multiple parties something they have 'shared' is, to say the least, inaccurate. An experience of war isn't commonly shared by both sides, nor is an outbreak of mass violence shared between one self-designated group and another: they can be discussed, common experiences exchanged, and attempts at atonement made, but to call the aftermath of war or ethnic cleansing a shared cultural history between all parties involved is to iron history into meaninglessness. Racial and cultural communities that share a fairly uniform history can arrive at an idea of shared, internalized hatred, but South Asians in the diaspora don't have a firm, united past: their ancestors are on separate sides of the borders of countries, classes, and wars.

Just as curry doesn't exactly exist, neither does the diasporic South Asian. If we're attempting to build solidarity out of a shared history, it will never quite mesh, hold true, unless our great-grandparents happen to be from the same time and place. And even – perhaps especially – in a cosmopolitan city like Toronto, there's every chance that the diasporic people I meet emerge from a past unlike my own genetic-historical soup of coolies, office clerks, a security guard, an auctioneer, a psychiatric nurse, and an ophthalmologist. Members of Team Diaspora may have skin of the same general tone, but each has a recent family history that is likely completely distinct.

As a collective, South Asians in the West are bound by the incredible range of possible origins they might have had, the unknowability of their pasts, and the comical accident of resemblance. 'There are so many pockets across the world with an Indo-centric definition,' Róisín goes on to write, 'and brown kids from Brampton might have nothing in common with the brown kids in Heathrow, yet the echo of the undefined territory booms louder than our shared similarities.' This undefined territory she's referring to – 'what it means to be South Asian in the West' – is perhaps impossible and undesirable to bridge: why define a uniform way of being, of existing as a brown mass in the West, in reaction to our perceived resemblance to each other and the cultural overlaps that diasporic people do share?

When discussing past South Asian conflicts, our sometimes-fatal inability to get along in the centuries of the past, the collective 'we,' the 'us,' sounds right because the idea of a vast South Asian collective makes sense. 'We' also makes sense when we're talking about some of what we do share as diasporic subjects: great swaths of cultural artifacts and attitudes, lots of food, and the fact that we're perceived as part of the same mass, one that we've gradually unified under for the sake of political, academic, and cultural advocacy. The key to defining diasporic South Asian identity isn't letting go of or healing the past: it's in stridently resisting definition, the idea that we should have to tell stories that reflect the shared, collective experience of what is in reality an incredibly diverse category of individuals from complicated, different pasts and places. But in the West, brown people are perceived as being on the same racial team and, in fact, many brown people do feel that that's exactly true, as Róisín seems to when she sees 'us, not an appropriative version of us' in *Bend It Like Beckham*.

Inventing a shared past to create a unified diasporic culture is, in part, the project of currybooks, of narratives such as *Bend It Like Beckham*, which are built on easily recognizable touch-stone tropes. But the past can't be altered to fit a desire for belonging and solidarity in the present: what people in the South Asian diaspora in the West share is that people looking at us assume that we all come from a similar past and place. But we don't, and there's no need to pretend that we do.

I've always found *Bend It Like Beckham* to be a shallow parade of annoying stereotypes of older-generation South Asian stiffness and their grudgingly dutiful, big-dreamin' children. I also understand that I'm not at all the target audience, and understood that I wasn't anywhere close to the target demographic when I saw the film in the Park Theatre in

Vancouver at age twenty, alongside my equally bored and annoyed father. It was precisely the placating notions of unity and shared experience that bothered me about the movie. The cut-out parents, in particular, with their finger-wagging admonitions barely exceeding the character development in a Twisted Sister music video until the inevitable, predictable, third-act relinquishment of tradition and acceptance of their daughter's personhood, frustrated me in their prêt-à-porter relatability. But the film's impact on brown girls and women who saw their own wishes to escape cultural expectations is undeniable – and, as Rajpreet Heir wrote in the *Atlantic*, director Gurinder Chadha works to create a sense of hybrid identity in protagonist Jess, played by Parminder Nagra:

> In showing Jess in so many traditional situations – making Indian food, dancing at her sister's wedding ceremonies, and trying to wrap a pink sari in the locker room – alongside the scenes of her trying to pursue football, *Bend It Like Beckham* helps viewers better understand Jess's masterpiece invention of a hybrid identity … To play soccer in the park with the boys and then secretly play for a team, while also trying to be a good Indian daughter, requires nonstop maneuvering.

I didn't even come close to noticing this about *Bend*, but upon rewatching, I can't disagree with Heir, and have to acknowledge the reactionary nature of my analysis of the film as it exists in my memories. Despite the hammier aspects of the film around her, particularly her strident 'Respect your elders!' parents, the hybridity of Jess's identity is delicately and cleverly depicted. As much as I like to hope that my critical skills have some degree of purity, my response to *Bend* is entirely in line with my earlier resistance to reading diasporic novels simply because they were diasporic novels. But I'm more sympathetic to my post-adolescent reaction to *Beckham*:

a packaged version of what it's like to be a non-traditional brown person in the West agitating against old-fashioned parents was something I had every right to be utterly disinterested in. *Bend It Like Beckham* arrived at my eyes as part of an old genre, a descendant of *Footloose* and *Pump Up the Volume*, the racial and cultural elements decorations on a story I'd seen many times. A story like this adjusting itself to Western contours – the teen rebellion movie browned and bangled – truly did mean something to brown teenagers and kids who it hit at the right time. But the film's power isn't in how fresh and South Asian it is, but in how familiar and Western it is. It casts people of a relatable colour in a narrative that was previously just-for-whites: while *Bend* doesn't say anything profound about South Asian culture, and likely didn't intend to, the movie does say something to secular South Asian teenagers in the West – that their struggles are analogous to the ones they've seen in white, Hollywood narratives. Like so many stories of rebellion, this is a movie about discovering you're just like everyone else, and that's okay. It shares this with *Harold & Kumar Go to White Castle*: both films are mainstreaming narratives, stories that don't efface the unique aspects of diasporic experience, but do concentrate on just how Western brown people in the West can be.

There's ingrained colonialism and empire in the mere existence of any brown narrative written or filmed in a non-Indian language: for the ones in English, the connection is inescapable. Indian diasporic writers and a large proportion of Indian writers, whether they stayed on in the country or not, seized this linguistic tool for expression, recognition, and financial betterment with resounding results, from *Midnight's Children* to *The God of Small Things* to *Narcopolis*. When I was a teenager listening to death metal and black metal, I wondered why these Nordic Europeans sang in English. As an adult listening to death metal and black metal and reading diasporic literature, the question rarely occurs to me: you write in English because you have to, because history and movement have rendered your mother tongue a novelty. Or, crucially, because you don't have a mother tongue – you never learned it from your mother, or maybe she didn't from hers. Either way, writing in an Indian language would shrink your market, and if you're second-gen, you'd likely never come close to the fluency you have in the language that arrived at your tongue courtesy of historical and economic machinations that didn't pause to ask what you wanted to speak.

Wealth is another pervasive, although often hidden, actor in this genre stream in South Asian narratives: these memoirs, novels, films, and stand-up comedy acts are most often written by the wealthy, or at least the middle classes. The kind of people whose families had servants in the old country, perhaps, and who regenerated wealth in the new one. As I heard at many a family-friend dinner party growing up, this rebuilding of class status and money often wasn't easy, with the transfer of educational and professional credentials from the subcontinent to the West rarely being straightforward. The fall from the past in a diasporic story is often also a fall in signifiers of everyday comfort, as in Kiran Desai's *The Inheritance of Loss*, where rural cook's son Biju embarks on what he thinks of as a trip upward, living as an illegal immigrant in New York City. Instead, he lives in horrible conditions, contending with rats running over his sleeping body by night as he works for minuscule wages by day.

While deceptive portrayals of a better life in the West (and often direct lies about the fortunes that await across the ocean) have propelled emigration for decades past, a longing for escape to the West is a staple of many real-life immigrant stories. In *Lion*, for example, Saroo's wresting from his family also uplifts him into economic circumstances that would likely have been far beyond his reach had he stayed in his homeland. In Hari

Kunzru's 2004 novel *Transmission*, Indian programmer Arjun Mehta is deceived with prospects of a job that matches his vision of a luxurious life in the West, but ends up working in contract-employee servitude, barely scraping by and at the mercy of employers who could cut them loose at any time. What fuels Arjun's move is a vision of life in a permissive society where companionship and bounty are a given:

> His current favorite daydream was set in a mall, a cavern of bright glass through which a near-future version of himself was traveling at speed up a broad, black escalator. Dressed in a button-down shirt and a baseball cap with the logo of a major software corporation embroidered on the peak, Future-Arjun was holding hands with a young woman who looked not unlike Kajol, his current filmi crush. As Kajol smiled at him, the compact headphones in his ears transmitted another upbeat love song, just one of the never-ending library of new music stored in the tiny MP3 player on his belt.

Abandoning actual India for a false vision of America proves to be a mistake for Arjun, who sinks into increasingly depressing work situations and eventually becomes a fugitive from justice. But this downward trajectory isn't always the story: for diasporic hoppers such as my parents and many of their friends in the U.K. and Canada, the nursing professors and the software successes and the business people, it worked out. Some visit back-home more than others (back-home ranging from Guyana to Mauritius to Gujarat), but I don't think any of them seriously entertain the idea of moving back for good. And, almost certainly, they wouldn't reconsider having emigrated in the first place: the elements that they miss, they can go back for, or simply feel nostalgic for. What would have been missed by not leaving is their lives: the substance of their careers, the families they made, their existence itself. Diaspora

worked out better for some than for others – much better –
but the success stories complicate feelings of longing for the
past and a different land. But that's fine – stories and literature
are methods we have for dealing with complexities.

When such complexity is calcified into clichéd tropes, it
becomes simplified and rote. British journalist Bidisha was
asked to speak at an event on Indian literature and languages
at the 2016 London Book Fair. Writing about the event afterwards, she called attention to repeating narratives:

> the forbidden romance between the Mughal princess and the
> servant boy in a lotus garden; English stiff upper lips melting in
> the heat of the Empire's monsoon season; the fraught narratives
> of being tempted by religious fundamentalism or condemned
> to a forced marriage, of struggling to survive destitution and
> poverty, of being torn between parental tradition and youthful
> self-determination, the clichés of cruel brown men and suffering
> brown women, vast differences of equality and opportunity,
> the agonies of culture and identity. These things do happen,
> but they are not the only stories.

Not the only stories, indeed. I'm sure Bidisha would agree
that novels and collections appear every year that push against
the edges of these stories, exceed or ignore them completely,
but the sheer percentage mass of repeating stories in the field
of South Asian letters is impossible to ignore. Her prescription
for the future involves a loosening of strictures on what
authors are expected to produce, even defying these expectations outright and defending 'our inclinations as artists who
are Indian, or Indian diaspora, or second- or third-generation
writers of Indian heritage living far from the birthplace of our
grandparents. We have as much right to produce a bourgeois
comedy of manners, a psychological thriller or a ripping space
opera as we do to craft realistic, sober literary fiction.'

Even within that category of realistic, sober literary fiction, South Asians diasporic and otherwise encounter a restriction, which novelist Rumaan Alam indicates in his review of Rakesh Satyal's *No One Can Pronounce My Name*: 'There is a tendency to presume autobiography in fiction by women or minorities. Guys named Jonathan write *universal* stories, while there's this sense that everyone else is just fictionalizing their own, small experiences. That can be charming but it doesn't approach *importance*.' Race and cultural background are inextricable from an author's life, experience, knowledge of other people – but the empathetic, individual, *particular* vision that is the value of any good literary effort must be allowed to look outward, must be given permission to rove outside of the parameters of experience that other books have convinced you that an author with a brown-sounding name is allowed to have.

Bidisha trains her critique of what brown writers are allowed to produce on the white-dominated world of U.K. publishing – she was addressing them directly at the London Book Fair – but her words would be just as apt in a much wider context of not just publishers, but readers. The modes of expression available to brown writers may be dictated by the industry's commitment to the immediately marketable, but also by what readers of all races are interested in reading.

My own hubristic crime as a young reader, skipping over the brown-name books on my parents' shelves, was not believing that particularity could exist in any of those books, that they could be anything other than versions of each other – and later, while writing, that I'd only find what I wanted to write about in flight from the stories that other brown writers were supposed to tell, when really I did want to write about race, about culture, about family – just my own particular version of it, which seemed utterly out of step with what I found in the sari- or-mango-on-the-cover books.

While these straight-up, mango-gnawing examples of

currybooks certainly exist – those homecoming-comfort-authenticity blends that present a packaged version of what it is to be a disconnected brown person in the West – finding exactly what I was looking for when I began researching them intently was harder than I thought. That base blend I describe was certainly present in many books, but I was surprised by how many of them – Lahiri's *The Namesake*, Ali's *Brick Lane* – had markedly excellent qualities, weren't just show-and-tell roadside zoos of exoticism and alienation. The broad emotional and cultural notes being struck, of an over-there and back-then being absent from a central character's existence, resonated strongly in many of these books, but it didn't make them all hackwork. When the genre is explored by thoughtful writers with unique insights, the result is a quality book – which makes it all the more difficult to step outside this genre as a brown writer. Still, there are also books by brown people that riff on the tropes without surrendering to them. Often, they have the same kind of fruit-and-silk-adorned covers, but books such as Canadian writer Pasha Malla's recent *Fugue States* do something to eke out more space for stories unburdened by the tropes of the currybook. As Malla told Aparita Bhandari at *NOW Magazine*, his return-to-Kashmir novel explores a homecoming that isn't a plunge into the past, but into the realities of socio-political change:

'The character [Brij] in my book is based a little bit on my father,' explains Malla. 'My father was able to go back to Kashmir. But for Brij, the inability to go back creates an identity around the place that's rarefied. And for Ash, Kashmir has become a fantasy land that exists only in stories.

'The book is an exploration of how identity – not just national but personal, gender, political – is created through storytelling … writing this book I was owning the clichés in order to undermine them.

'The whole first generation seeking their roots from trauma is a problematic story. It's a solipsistic way of understanding trauma … By eventually forcing the character into it, and by undermining the script, I wanted to illustrate the falseness of those stories.'

Malla's previous work successfully evaded addressing the clichés: in the story collection and novel preceding *Fugue States*, Malla had sidestepped the curry game completely, delivering closely observed and sometimes surreal character-based stories that had little to do with his racial or cultural origin. In the same interview, he describes avoiding writing about his identity partially in reaction to the way 'South Asian writing is commod-ified … Writers of colour are expected to explain themselves to a larger [read white] [interviewer's insertion] audience … I was not comfortable participating in that mechanism.' Malla's interviewer, Bhandari, herself of South Asian heritage, transi-tions from this quotation by writing that in *Fugue States* 'Malla finally decided to explore his heritage.' That 'finally,' from a brown reader and writer, is telling – it's not just the majority-white audience that anticipates identity- and heritage-focused stories from brown novelists and memoirists: it's the brown audience, too. Bhandari's interest in this novel that, as she writes, confronts 'tropes and archetypes head on' also points to an eagerness on the brown (and, I'd argue, much of the white) audience's part to read different stories, to have their expectations that a novel by a brown writer is going to be all about heritage, about looking back to the homeland, frustrated.

Nostalgia fuels everything from revivalist rock to right-wing political movements. As American political scientist Mark Lilla has pointed out, European nationalists, the Amer-ican right, and extremist Islamist organizations all embed a vision of life lived better in the past in their vision of the future. South Asian immigrant fiction, memoir, and cookbooks

– all of them contributors to the currybook genre – are often deeply marked by nostalgia, by a drive for discovering the authenticity left behind in another time and place. South Asian Writer is an identity, not just a pair of adjectives and a noun: and it's an identity that establishes a tacit promise to an audience that is seeking it, whether the author intended it or not. What's promised? Authenticity, a sense of the past, of a realer elsewhere.

As Changez, the narrator of Mohsin Hamid's brilliant 2007 novel-in-monologue-form *The Reluctant Fundamentalist*, realizes in post-9/11 Manhattan, looking back has become part of the cultural order of Western life. As the foundations of his American existence begin to fracture beneath him, he notices everyone around him looking backwards, to a past where he may not belong – it's only natural that his own gaze, later in the novel, will become fixated on the rear-view.

Possibly this was due to my state of mind, but it seemed to me that America, too, was increasingly giving itself over to a dangerous nostalgia at that time. There was something undeniably retro about the flags and uniforms, about generals addressing cameras in war rooms and newspaper headlines featuring such words as *duty* and *honor*. I had always thought of America as a nation that looked forward; for the first time I was struck by its determination to look *back*. Living in New York was suddenly like living in a film about the Second World War; I, a foreigner, found myself staring out at a set that ought to be viewed not in Technicolor but in grainy black and white. What your fellow countrymen longed for was unclear to me – a time of unquestioned dominance? of safety? of moral certainty? I did not know – but that they were scrambling to don the costumes of another era was apparent. I felt treacherous for wondering whether that era was fictitious, and whether – if it could indeed be animated – it contained a part for someone written like me.

It feels unnecessary to belabour the 'Make America Great Again' overtones to the America that Changez sees, but what's perhaps slightly less evident is the role that Changez has found and that he plays throughout the novel: he is narrating his past, in this long monologue, to an American in the Old Anarkali district of Lahore, Pakistan. That is the part written for him – to discuss the mistake of thinking he had a place in America, and the story of his voyage to the homeland. Hamid is riffing on the currybook, too, without directly acknowledging its touchstones. In this story of a young, successful Pakistani who can't find happiness or a place in America, against a backdrop of terrorism, menace, and everyday racism, Hamid crafts a sinister homecoming, a nostalgia imposed from the outside that drives his protagonist back to the nation where he came from, and makes storytelling and visitations into the past itself a charged weapon against the American who is hearing his story in a state of heightened alertness and fear. As Changez points out, nostalgia can be 'dangerous.' It's not just classic rock and vanilla milkshakes: it's a close ally of extremism and racism in America, Pakistan, and the rest of the world.

The restricted stories of brown homecoming and nostalgia that form the tropes and clichés of currybooks don't reflect the variegated, class-divided, and culturally widespread experiences of brown people in the West. They present a comforting, streamlined, and largely untrue version of what brown people were and are, to a multiracial audience of readers who are supposed to recognize themselves or their neighbours. They also continually point to the fact that brown people aren't *from* the West, even if they live in the West, even if they were born in the West. A link to one's genealogical and geographical roots can be fulfilling and enriching, but when it's imposed on you from the outside that you're supposed to know and tell these roots, to be able to present the papers that explain your skin to a waiting audience, the homecoming trip feels a little less heartwarming.

Samad Iqbal, a character in Zadie Smith's 2000 domestic-cultural epic novel *White Teeth*, carries out the project that Chanu in Monica Ali's *Brick Lane* intended: he brings his offspring back to Bangladesh. Chanu, alone in the old country, peacefully comes to the never-the-same-river-twice realization that his homeland was never the place he remembered it as, and it certainly isn't the wish-fulfillment he expected when he returns. He's still himself, in a place that is almost as new to him as England was when he emigrated. Smith's Samad brings Magid, one of his twin sons, back to Bangladesh. Instead of Samad having produced a tradition-steeped, pious son, Magid becomes an atheist, a scientist, a lover of the modern world. The twin who stays in England, Millat, is the one who has the serious flirtation with fundamentalism and the past, joining a rugged Islamist cult that perpetrates minor acts of terrorism. In keeping with Mark Lilla's averment that extremism and nostalgia are intimately connected, Millat's slide into fundamentalism is made possible by his unfamiliarity with the realities of his homeland in combination with his discontentment with London life. His twin has actually made the trip back: the ultimate disillusionment, the actual, inevitably disappointing enactment of homecoming.

A poisonous, crucial element of this imposed expectation is that brown people and their books should look back, into a past and a place that may never have existed. Ash, Malla's protagonist in *Fugue States*, is also a writer, and his second novel 'was supposed to have been "about Kashmir,"' but his 'inability to invent characters, resistance to research, misgivings about treating tenuous cultural heritage as *material*' prevent him from ever starting this novel. Ash's father offers his son comments on his attempt at a short story set in Kashmir, remarking on just how many details his son has gotten wrong, from people keeping dogs as pets during the worst of the Troubles to the inclusion of non-existent cobblestoned streets. 'You have made the city vague. You have missed its particulars. Where is Dal Lake? One must either go to Kashmir so one might write something accurate or one must write about some place one has been and knows. One has a debt to the people of any forgotten or ignored place.'

Brij, a reader with stern expectations of what a book about the homeland should do, may have it right when he talks about the debt a writer owes to the real people who live in the real places he or she writes about: but does this have anything to do with the invisible contract the writer has with the reader? Ash's (likely bad) short story about Kashmir could still do something for its audience: it would show the disconnected, racialized writer questing for truth in the past, even if he is inventing that past and place as he feels it out. As Ash considers a trip to Kashmir after his father's death and the discovery that Brij left an unfinished novel of his own behind, he constantly feels warded off by the burden of cliché, by the pressure of the unseen, page-flipping audience: 'Besides: brown boy's dad dies, brown boy flees to the fatherland to discover who he really is? No thanks. I've seen that movie and it sucks.' And: 'Picture it: me scattering the cremains from some mountain, and then honoring his memory by completing the opus. And then what? People read it and are so moved that peace descends on the valley? Or worse, I win a prize?'

The valley, Kashmir, is part of the audience that Ash imagines, with the prize jab denoting the white literary establishment over in this hemisphere. It's a broad crowd to imagine 'explaining' oneself to: and this is the expectation that Malla told his interviewer he sees imposed on books by South Asian writers. Opening the audience question both ways, as his character does, making writing by South Asians an explanation of Westernized brown people to the East, and an explanation of brownness and the eternal truths of the tumultuous homeland to the West, shows just how multivalent a set of coded clichés can be. Telling the same story of brownness over and over doesn't only express a coherent notion of race and history to white readers, it creates an impression of commonalities among a brown audience who may come from vastly divided pasts and have little in common in their present, other than they 'all look the same' in communities where they're part of a box-tick minority category.

There are near-infinite tellings of South Asian experience possible, a library labyrinth of potential novels about everything from white serial killers to brown university janitors. It's just that accepting that diasporic identity is as slippery as personal identity is as thrilling, daunting, and worryingly progressive as acknowledging the total unpredictability of the future and the lack of comfort to be found in the past.

A few years ago, I wrote a story that splinted the fragile ankles of my writing career and pushed me into the world of professionalized writing. I hate getting annoyingly mystical about writing crap, and I will try to avoid it here, but completing this story was the first time that I felt, truly, that I'd written something good. Ray Bradbury often retold the experience of completing his early story 'The Lake': 'When I finished the short story, I burst into tears. I realized that after ten years of writing, I'd finally written something beautiful.' Thank Christ, I can say that I didn't cry or come anywhere close when I finished writing my first good story. I just felt helpless and beaten.

If this story wasn't good enough to leap the rejection pile, if it wasn't good enough to do something to confirm that my writing wasn't just a shadow-puppet show in a lightless room, it was time to stop. The piece was both the best I could do and something I'd never done before: a story set in Mauritius. I called it 'Cinema Rex,' geographically cheating the location of the movie theatre next to the house where my father had grown up in the fifties – the one next to him was actually called the Majestic, but I couldn't risk an earnest Jim Carrey sneaking into my phantom reader's mind. I was twenty-nine and felt depleted by the steady lack of success that typically characterizes the early days of building a writing career. So I took what I told myself was a last shot, with a mixture of repugnant self-pity and genuine hopelessness. I put a story in an envelope and mailed it in to a small literary journal contest.

The force of the idea as it came to me – the boy who lived next to the movie theatre, a portal into a world he wanted to live in, rooted in a place that was trying to hold on to him – felt strong, insistent. As I wrote it out, I felt free of any of the critical doubts I've voiced in this book about retreading stories of homecoming, of the homeland, of the past. I knew the shape of the story and what the characters would be doing, and I knew it had more power than most of the scribbling I'd been doing for the past couple of years. Revising it, I knew that it could be received as a currybook-style narrative, but I thought that it was so clearly about a nostalgia-free escape that it was clad against that reading. Wasn't it?

'Cinema Rex' is at the upper end of short-story length and the lower end of novella, with the on-page text telling the story of three boys attending Rex's opening-night screening of *The Night of the Hunter*. I was arrested by the idea of a boy growing up next door to a movie theatre and seeing it as a portal into the West, and aligning past and future timelines on the same page to create a sense of each character's future informing his past. Footnotes leap the reader forward in time, showing the future film careers, deaths, successes, and failures of the boys, two of whom manage to escape Mauritius. That's where my story strayed from the tropes, I told myself after it was finished: these boys want *out*, they have as much desire to stay on the island as Clint Eastwood had to remain on Alcatraz, as I had to keep living in Kelowna. They seek a way out of their childhoods through the screen, and they make their escape without wistfully looking back.

But the fucking *story itself* is a look back. I was flirting with the currybook genre and its tropes simply by having the background I do, drawing on the familial background that I did, and casting a narrative line into a past and setting that are as exotic to me as they are familiar to my parents. Nostalgia is inextricable from a story about leaving the homeland, which means my story is open to the same kind of interpretive lens I've put on work by South Asian writers throughout this book. When 'Cinema Rex' won one prize and then another, and agents and publishers communicated their interest in me for the first time, I thought I'd expand the story, fill in the interstices between the past and those footnotes, arriving at a full depiction of what became of these kids from the fifties through the nineties, a novel spanning that Mauritian cinema, London squats in '68, rent-boy life in 1970s Rome for a brown film composer both hiding and using his race, right up to the grotesqueries of 1980s Hollywood. I drafted most of it, showing no one, and received a fair amount of book-industry interest in my inbox and at events, a murmur that has never completely abated.

But a general – while certainly not universal – lack of interest in anything else or anyone else that I was writing about alerted me that I was at risk. Publishers and agents who were initially intrigued that I wrote crime fiction and that many of my other short stories were about contemporary people of various races and social classes, rarely with a South Asian central character, had little interest in that work once they actually saw it. They wanted, it seemed to me, the brown nostalgia book, the one that fit a slot in the publication schedule for readers who like buying that sort of thing.

In Canada, which has a literary industry supported strongly by arts grants and a healthy prize culture funded largely by private and corporate donors, there may be a particular relationship to publishing a currybook. Prominent on my familial shelves when I was growing up were two novels by Mumbai-born, Canadian-settled Rohinton Mistry: 1991's *Such a Long Journey* and 1995's *A Fine Balance*. International hits of the highest order, with accolades from the Booker shortlist to Oprah's Book Club, Mistry's brown success in Canada at that time was outstripped only by Sri Lankan–born Michael Ondaatje, whose own eighties and nineties megahits *In the Skin of a Lion* and *The English Patient* strayed from any blueprint of brown writing by centring on characters of varying races with no geographical link to the author's country of origin. Mistry's big books were Indian-set, and were the high-visibility descendants of novels by South Asian-Canadian authors such as Bharati Mukherjee, whose earliest works centred on ethnic identity and alienation in the West. Mistry's novels, rooted as they were in India, embedded looking-back as part of the successful narrative of diasporic writing in this country, especially when his success became international.

In a small literary culture fuelled by publishers seeking material with a trackable success record and granting agencies with juries who may tend to favour riffs on what they've read before, pieces of writing that strum familiar chords tend to rise to the top. My currybook anxiety is justified: being so invested in avoiding the tropes means some brown writers, like me, or Pasha Malla, may end up tripping over them to the detriment of our own ability to tell our particular stories or, at least, to get them published. What they're interested in up here in Canada, it seems – at least, it can seem when you're sending that email to a journal or an agent or a publisher – has a lot to do with how you write about where you ultimately came from, and not about what you write about as a brown Westerner with a collection of different interests and experiences.

Diasporic South Asians appear in much of my work, and my experience pervades all of it. But I suspect that many of the few who read me wonder where my *identity* is, my struggles with belonging, ethnicity, and dislocation. That's why I can't ever be completely lighthearted about currybooks: they teach us to predict the contents of what we are about to read, and they prescribe the limits of what we are – of what I am – supposed to publish.

While my decision to write thrillers under the pseudonym I made up when I was fourteen – basing the last name on Sigourney Weaver's character in *Alien* and the first on the simplest WASP analogue of my name – came from my desire to write crime and horror fiction alongside my literary fiction, to have two simultaneous careers like Iain Banks or John Banville, I knew the audience could see it another way. They could interpret me as trading one genre for another, avoiding the currybooks that would come 'naturally' to me by assuming an identity that I could write anything from – a white identity. Thrillers, at least the kind that I want to continue writing, offer something wonderful to writers: you're supposed to defy the conventions that you flirt with; you're supposed to endlessly surprise the reader, to lead them into the unfamiliar. This, of course, is something that can be said of high literary novels, as well – they're meant to initiate us into an experience of the unfamiliar, or a different experience of something we believe we've felt or done before. I have confidence that the readers of my thriller fiction want unfamiliarity from me, and that gives me great pleasure.

Pseudonymous writers like Stephen King (Richard Bachman), Donald E. Westlake (Richard Stark), John Banville (Benjamin Black), and Julian Barnes (Dan Kavanagh) used their other names for various reasons: King to publish at the rate he was writing, and to test whether he could still sell under another name; Banville to indicate to his following of literary readers that his detective fiction was a different thing altogether, and also to create another persona, one who could write much faster than his literary self. I feel the same as he does about the actual creative process, though he's more willing to credit the mystical. As he wrote in the *Guardian*: 'When I stand up from my writing desk, "John Banville," or "Benjamin Black" – that is, the one whose name will appear on the title page – vanishes on the instant, since he only existed while the writing was being done.' Banville has his Booker Prize–winning, high-lit reputation to think of, and escape from, when he's writing as Black. Am I escaping the expectations of what a brown writer is supposed to make when I write as Ripley? I'd be lying if I said I hadn't thought about it, but I'd also be lying if I said it ever occurred to me when I was actually writing. And I know that while my pseudonym can vanish when I stand up from my laptop, my racial and cultural identity will never separate themselves from the name Naben Ruthnum on any title page or cover that I have the fortune to arrive at: not to an audience and a business that retains a fixation on the writer's identity, on how it lends gravity to the story that is being told in the pages to follow.

A couple of years after standing up from the desk (actually a small TV table in my Vancouver bedroom) where I wrote 'Cinema Rex,' I found agents who liked all of what I did. We sold the thriller I'd written to an American publisher. ('Cinema Rex' had attracted as much notice as a short story in a Canadian literary journal can be expected to draw in the States.) After that novel sold, I had to acknowledge that it was possible I'd imagined industry disinterest in the work I'd done that strayed from the field of brown nostalgia, that I was being prematurely bitter, or that much of my other writing didn't measure up to whatever promise people saw in 'Cinema Rex.' I kept having stories published, with certain editors and magazines clearly not caring what I was writing about, as long as the pieces were good. Writing that story had made me better at writing whatever came next – in a true currybook narrative, this would be thanks to me finally writing about my heritage, to discovering what made my voice worth hearing. But that's not it – once you've written something you truly believe is good, you keep working to match and exceed it, not to recreate its reception or the formal elements that went into it. The story's value to me was its quality, not its setting.

When I discussed my career anxieties with a writer friend a couple years back, he faked together portions of a nightmare essay that pinpointed my fears of what people would think of my pen-name decision:

Like much of Ruthnum's writing, his thriller deals with a man's conflicting inner and outer lives, where the protagonist spends most of his time fretting the veil is going to be lifted. (The reason most of Ruthnum's work is so often redolent of the pulp style is because its built-in requirement for duplicity allows him to explore his identity issues while masked in tradition.) The purpose of Ruthnum's employment of 'Ripley' as the author of this latest novel (which is larger in scope and scale than 'Cinema Rex') is twofold. One is to efface Ruthnum's identity, CV, and previous publications (including 'Rex') as a whole, and two is to supersede that work with one that is more true to who Naben/Nathan really is.

A large portion of the 'Cinema Rex' novel exists – enough that I could complete some version of it, could give it a shot on the market. I can't honestly say it would be good, though. Trigger-shyness started to overwhelm me as I moved deeper into writing it, realizing with some horror that I might be guilty of nostalgia – not for a lost homeland that I never knew, but for a story I'd already told. I couldn't risk making this novel what readers saw from me first. I would never be able to believe that it was published because of the book it was, and not the nostalgia-and-authenticity genre trip that it was capable of delivering once it left my laptop and reached eyes that aren't my own. The only way I could be absolutely sure I wasn't starting with a currybook was by starting with this, a book called *Curry*, which in so many ways plays by the genre rules. It has recipes, memories of my mother and father, a trip to an exotic country of origin, infinite mangoes, alienation and dislocation, and even a realization: that I fear this genre because I fear internalizing the outside pressure to create and enjoy the story that you want to read.

The associations that come with the South Asian Writer designation – the tropes that make us easy to group together on a table with a sign reading *Subcontinental Sojourn* in a big-box bookstore – are the recurring narrative patterns I've always tried to avoid. Categorization – the same industry- and consumer-focused drive that allowed Indian restaurants and the late-twentieth-century variation on the eternally change-able curry to thrive – has a role in the stratification of the South Asian immigrant novel, in the delimiting of what these books can be. Particularity doesn't market as easily as famil-iarity: hence the drive for a South Asian experience that can be defined, replicated, and sold as a comfortable reflection of lived experience. What's lost? Thanks to writers from V. S. Naipaul to Jade Sharma, who ignore the exigencies of catego-rization and the smoother path to publication that it offers, perhaps very little. Stories of particularity, of individual expe-rience emerging from an undefined South Asian experience, continue to emerge.

But there must be other stories that are lost, or go unread, because of the dominance of the story we've heard before.

Ali, Monica. *Brick Lane*. New York: Scribner, 2003.

Adichie, Chimamanda Ngozi. 'The Danger of a Single Story,' *TED.com*. Speech posted Oct 7, 2009.

Akhtar, Jabeen. 'Why Am I Brown? South Asian Fiction and Pandering to Western Audiences.' *Los Angeles Review of Books*, September 20, 2014.

——.'The 17 Elements of a (Bad) South Asian Novel.' *Publishing Perspectives*, June 24, 2014.

Alam, Rumaan. 'What Should the Indian-American Novel Be?' *The New Republic*, May 1, 2017.

Al-Solaylee, Kamal. *Brown: What Being Brown in the World Today Means (to Everyone)*. Toronto: HarperCollins, 2016.

Ansari, Aziz and Alan Yang (Creators). *Master of None*, Netflix, 2015.

Banville, John. 'John Banville on the birth of his dark twin, Benjamin Black.' *The Guardian*, July 22, 2011.

Barnes, Julian. *The Pedant in the Kitchen*. London: Atlantic, 2013.

Bhandari, Aparita. 'Pasha Malla: "Writers of colour are expected to explain themselves to a larger audience."' *NOW Magazine*, June 6, 2017.

Bidisha. 'The Great Contradiction.' *TLS*, March 20, 2017.

Bittman, Mark. *The Best Recipes in the World: More Than 1,000 International Dishes to Cook at Home*. New York: Broadway, 2005.

Bourdain, Anthony. *Kitchen Confidential: Adventures in the Culinary Underbelly*. New York: Harper Perennial, 2007.

Buford, Bill. *Heat: An Amateur's Adventures As Kitchen Slave, Line Cook, Pasta Maker, and Apprentice to a Dante-Quoting Butcher in Tuscany*. New York: Knopf, 2006.

Cameron, James. *An Indian Summer*. London: Macmillan, 1974.

Chaudhuri, Amit. *Calcutta: Two Years in the City*. New York: Vintage, 2015.

Chef Arfan Razak (Raz) Showreel, YouTube, April 27, 2012.

'Chicken Tikka Masala.' *In Search of Perfection*, BBC, October 16, 2007.

Collingham, E M. *Curry: A Tale of Cooks and Conquerors*. Oxford: Oxford University Press, 2007.

Collins, Ben. 'Dan Nainan, The Internet's Favorite "Millennial," is 55 Years Old.' *The Daily Beast*, May 1 2017.

'Curry Lounge, The.' *Ramsay's Kitchen Nightmares*, Channel 4, December 11, 2007.

David, Elizabeth. *French Provincial Cooking*. Illustrated by Juliet Renny. Harmondsworth: Penguin, 1964.

——.*English Bread and Yeast Cookery*. London: Penguin, 1977.

——.*A Book of Mediterranean Food*. Harmondsworth: Penguin, 1960.

Davis, Garth (Director). *Lion*. Australia / UK: See-Saw Films. Aquarius Films, Screen Australia Sunstar Entertainment, Cross City, The Weinstein Company. 2016.

Desai, Anita. *In Custody*. London: Penguin, 1988.

Desai, Kiran. *The Inheritance of Loss*. New York: Atlantic Monthly Press, 2005.

Dey, Ragini. *Spice Kitchen: Authentic Regional Indian Recipes to Recreate at Home*. Richmond: Hardie Grant, 2013.

Divakaruni, Chitra Banerjee. *Arranged Marriage: Stories*. New York: Doubleday, 1995.

——. *The Mistress of Spices*. New York: Anchor Books, 1997.

Duncan, Robert. *Masters of Fantasy: Ray Bradbury: An American Icon*. U.S.A.: Western International Communications Company, Atlantis Films. 1996.

Fisher, M. F. K. *The Gastronomical Me*. San Francisco: North Point Press, 1989.

Fitze, Kenneth S. *Twilight of the Maharajas (a Record of the Last Phase of Princely India)* [with Plates, Including Portraits.]. London: John Murray, 1956.

Ganeshananthan, V V. *Love Marriage*. New York: Random House, 2008.

Gilbert, Elizabeth. *Eat, Pray, Love: One Woman's Search for Everything Across Italy, India and Indonesia*. 10th Anniversary Edition. New York: Riverhead, 2016.

Gopnik, Adam. 'Dining Out.' *The New Yorker*, April 4, 2005.

Gowda, Shilpi Somaya. *The Golden Son*. New York: William Morrow, 2016.

Gunesekera, Romesh. *Reef*. London: Granta, 1994.

Hamid, Mohsin. *The Reluctant Fundamentalist*. Toronto: Random House of Canada, 2007.

Hariharan, Githa. *Almost Home: Finding a Place in the World from Kashmir to New York*. New York: Restless, 2016.

Heir, Rajpreet. 'Bend It Like Beckham and the Art of Balancing Cultures.' *The Atlantic*, April 12, 2017.

Kaling, Mindy (Creator). *The Mindy Project*, Fox, Hulu, 2012.

Kamal, Soniah. 'When My Authentic is Your Exotic.' *Literary Hub*, May 23, 2016.

Klein, Joshua. '"Harold & Kumar" breaks casting mold.' *The Chicago Tribune*. January 11, 2005.

Koul, Scaachi. 'There's No Recipe For Growing Up.' *BuzzFeed*, November 2, 2016.

Kureishi, Hanif. *The Buddha of Suburbia*. London: Faber & Faber, 1990.

Lahiri, Jhumpa. *In Other Words*. New York: Vintage, 2017.

——. 'The Long Way Home.' *The New Yorker*, September 6, 2004.

——. 'Rice.' *The New Yorker*, November 23, 2009.

Leiner, Danny (Director). *Harold & Kumar Go to White Castle*. U.S.A.: Senator International, Kingsgate Films, and Endgame Entertainment. 2004.

Lilla, Mark. *The Shipwrecked Mind: On Political Reaction*. New York: New York Review Books, 2016.

Lim, Dennis. 'Mining Post-9/11 America for Laughs.' *The New York Times*, April 20, 2008.

Liu, Karon. 'Meet Scarborough's unofficial food ambassador.' *Toronto Star*, May 18, 2016.

Malla, Pasha. *Fugue States*. Toronto: Knopf Canada, 2017.

Malladi, Amulya. *The Mango Season*. New York: Ballantine, 2013.

Marquand, Richard (Director). *Return of the Jedi: Episode VI*. U.S.A.: Lucasfilm Ltd, 1997.

Maxwell, Gavin. *A Reed Shaken by the Wind*. London: Longmans, Green, 1957.

McEwan, Ian. *The Comfort of Strangers*. London: Picador, 1983.

Mehta, Gita. *Karma Cola: Marketing the Mystic East*. New York: Vintage, 1994.

Mistry, Rohinton. *Such a Long Journey*. New York: Knopf, 1991.

——. *A Fine Balance*. New York: Vintage, 1995.

Mueenuddin, Daniyal. *In Other Rooms, Other Wonders*. New York: W. W. Norton & Co, 2009.

Nair, Kamala. *The Girl in the Garden*. New York: Grand Central Publishing, 2012.

Nair, Mira (Director). *Monsoon Wedding*. India / U.S.A. / Italy / France / Germany: Mirabai Films. 2001.

——. *The Namesake*. India / U.S.A.: Mirabai Films and UTV Motion Pictures. 2006.

Narayan, Shoba. *Monsoon Diary: A Memoir with Recipes*. New York: Random House, 2007.

O'Brian, Patrick. *The Mauritius Command*. New York: W. W. Norton & Company, 1977.

Ondaatje, Michael. *In the Skin of the Lion*. Toronto: McClelland and Stewart, 1987.

——. *The English Patient*. Toronto: Vintage Books of Canada, 1992.

Pathak, Meena. *Meena Pathak's Flavours of India*. London: New Holland, 2002.

Payne, Alexander (Director). *Sideways*. U.S.A.: Michael London Productions. 2004.

Permalloo, Shelina. *Sunshine on a Plate: Simple, Vibrant Cooking to Warm the Heart*. London: Ebury Press, 2013.

Pradhan, Monica. *The Hindi-Bindi Club*. London: Bloomsbury, 2008.

Rathi, Annada. 'The Problem With "Curry."' *Food52*, July 13, 2016.

Róisín, Fariha. 'Kids Like Us.' *Hazlitt*, April 11, 2017.

Roy, Sandip. *Don't Let Him Know*. New York: Bloomsbury, 2015.

Rushdie, Salman. *Imaginary Homelands: Essays and Criticism 1981–1991*. London: Granta, 1991.

——. 'After Midnight.' *Vanity Fair*, September, 1987: 88–94.

Smith, Zadie. *White Teeth*. London: Hamish Hamilton, 2000.

Sen, Mayukh. "How Indian Is Your 'Turmeric Latte'?" *Food52*, February 16, 2017.

Sodha, Meera, and David Loftus. *Made in India: Recipes from an Indian Family Kitchen*. New York: Flatiron Books, 2015.

Subramanian, Samanth. *Following Fish: Travels Around the Indian Coast*. London: Atlantic Books, 2014.

Vij, Vikram, and Meeru Dhalwala. *Vij's: Elegant & Inspired Indian Food*. Vancouver: Douglas & McIntyre, 2006.

Wright, Camron. *The Orphan Keeper*. Salt Lake City: Shadow Mountain, 2016.

Acknowledgements

Thanks to Rudrapriya Rathore, whose comments and conversation were crucial to the idea behind this book and the shape it eventually took.

To Emily Keeler, whose steady direction across the strange way we decided to compose this thing made it happen. And Alana Wilcox, Norman Nehmetallah, and Jessica Rattray of Coach House, who continue to push it onward.

To my reading family: Mandy, Kay, Sam, and Rouba Ruthnum, for teaching me the value in doing this at all.

My incomparable agents, Samantha Haywood and Stephanie Sinclair.

To Haley Cullingham and Miranda Hickman for teaching me how to write outside of fiction.

To Ian Worang, Daniel Reid, Leigh Doyle, Justin Reed, and Chris Hogg, for the backup I needed to get this project done.

And: Kris Bertin, Rob Inch, Buddy, Graeme Desrosiers, Aaron Peck, Michael LaPointe, Andrew Sullivan, Michael Haldane, Brad Iles, Mike Barrow, Kevin Keegan, Julia Cooper, Dan Moxon, Jon Bunyan, Ben Barootes, Gorrman Lee, Kate Zagorskis, Christopher Dingwall, David Bertrand, Charlotte Dykes, Kelli Korducki, Ashley MacCuish, Andrew Forbes, Carmine Starnino, Miranda Hill, Mark Medley, Russell Wangersky, Terence Young, Valerie Compton, Gabriella Goliger, Ben McGinnis, Kevin Chong, Jordan Christianson, Cody Hicks, Deborah Hemming, Joel Deshaye, Robin Feenstra, Ariel Buckley, Ian Whittington, Justin Pfefferle, Amanda Clarke, Paula Derdiger, Michelle Ledonne, Adèle Barclay, and Alicia Merchant.

About the Author

Naben Ruthnum won the Journey Prize for his short fiction, has been a *National Post* books columnist, and has written books and cultural criticism for the *Globe and Mail*, *Hazlitt*, and the *Walrus*. His crime fiction has appeared in *Ellery Queen's Mystery Magazine* and *Joyland*, and his pseudonym Nathan Ripley's first thriller, *Find You In The Dark*, will appear in 2018. Ruthnum lives in Toronto.

About the
Exploded Views Series

Exploded Views is a series of probing, provocative essays that offer surprising perspectives on the most intriguing cultural issues and figures of our day. Longer than a typical magazine article but shorter than a full-length book, these are punchy salvos written by some of North America's most lyrical journalists and critics. Spanning a variety of forms and genres – history, biography, polemic, commentary – and published simultaneously in all digital formats and handsome, collectible print editions, this is literary reportage that at once investigates, illuminates and intervenes.

www.chbooks.com/explodedviews

Typeset in Goodchild Pro and Gibson Pro. Goodchild was designed by Nick Shinn in 2002 at his ShinnType foundry in Orangeville, Ontario. Shinn's design takes its inspiration from French printer Nicholas Jenson who, at the height of the Renaissance in Venice, used the basic Carolingian minuscule calligraphic hand and classic roman inscriptional capitals to arrive at a typeface that produced a clear and even texture that most literate Europeans could read. Shinn's design captures the calligraphic feel of Jensen's early types in a more refined digital format. Gibson was designed by Rod McDonald in honour of John Gibson FGDC (1928–2011), Rod's long-time friend and one of the founders of the Society of Graphic Designers of Canada. It was McDonald's intention to design a solid, contemporary and affordable sans serif face.

Printed at the old Coach House on bpNichol Lane in Toronto, Ontario, on Rolland Opaque Natural paper, which was manufactured, acid-free, in Saint-Jérôme, Quebec, from 50 percent recycled paper, and it was printed with vegetable-based ink on a 1972 Heidelberg KORD offset litho press. Its pages were folded on a Baumfolder, gathered by hand, bound on a Sulby Auto-Minabinda and trimmed on a Polar single-knife cutter.

Series editor: Emily M. Keeler
Cover illustration by Chloe Cushman
Author photo by Ian Patterson

Coach House Books
80 bpNichol Lane
Toronto ON M5S 3J4
Canada

416 979 2217
800 367 6360

mail@chbooks.com
www.chbooks.co